and

CHURCHILL LIVINGSTONE NURSING TEXTS

Nutrition and Dietetics for Nurses
Sixth edition
Mary E. Beck

Principles of Infection and Immunity in Patient Care
Caroline Blackwell and D. M. Weir

Practical Therapeutics for Nursing and Related Professions
Third edition
James A. Boyle

Practical Notes on Nursing Procedures
Seventh edition
J. D. Britten

Bacteriology and Immunity for Nurses
Fifth edition
Ronald Hare and E. Mary Cooke

Drugs and Pharmacology for Nurses
Seventh edition
S. J. Hopkins

Essentials of Paediatrics for Nurses
Fifth edition
I. Kessel

Psychology as Applied to Nursing
Seventh edition
Andrew McGhie

A Nurse's Guide to Anaesthetics, Resuscitation and Intensive Care
Sixth edition
Walter Norris and D. Campbell

Anatomy and Physiology Applied to Nursing
Fifth edition
Janet T. E. Riddle

Principles of Nursing
Second edition
Nancy Roper

Foundations of Nursing and First Aid
Fifth edition
Janet S. Ross and Kathleen J. W. Wilson

Sociology and Nursing

James P. Smith
B Sc (Soc), DER, SRN, RNT, BTA Certificate, FRCN, FRSH,
District Nursing Officer, Brent Health District, London
Formerly Principal Nursing Officer (Education),
Hammersmith Hospital, London.
Patricia Chomley Orator, College of Nursing, Australia, 1979

SECOND EDITION

CHURCHILL LIVINGSTONE
EDINBURGH LONDON MELBOURNE AND NEW YORK 1981

CHURCHILL LIVINGSTONE
Medical Division of Longman Group Limited

Distributed in the United States of America by Churchill Livingstone Inc., 19 West 44th Street, New York, N.Y. 10036, and by associated companies, branches and representatives throughout the world.

First Edition 1976
Second Edition 1981

ISBN 0 443 02274 7

British Library Cataloguing in Publication Data

Smith, James P.
Sociology and nursing. – 2nd ed. – (Churchill Livingstone nursing text)
1. Sociology 2. Nursing – Social aspects
I. Title
301'.024'613 HM51

Printed in Hong Kong by Wah Cheong Printing Press Ltd

Preface to the Second Edition

I have been very pleased indeed to learn that *Sociology and Nursing* is being bought and read in several countries of the world, not only in Europe but also as far afield as the African continent, Australasia and North America. I hope this second edition will be as popular.

During the preparation of this edition I have paid careful attention to the many helpful comments I have received, particularly those written by reviewers in the journals. I think that most of them will find that they have influenced the content and structure of this new edition in one way or another. But, of course, it still reflects the author's perspective and I make no apology for that.

Without the continued help and support from the publishers and my secretary, Mrs Ann Weller, publications like this would not be possible. I thank them both. And I thank my many readers who have obviously demonstrated that they are interested in what I have to share with them.

London, 1980 J.P.S.

Preface to the First Edition

'We are all sociologists now in the sense that we recognise it is impossible to think purposefully about many contemporary problems without thinking about society' (A.K.C. Ottaway, 1962).

Increasing numbers of basic and post basic nursing students and other health care students are reading sociology now in schools of nursing and institutions of further and higher education. Rightly so, as sociology affords a perspective on health and illness as major social phenomena and also endows health care practitioners with a fuller understanding of, and richer insights into, the society in which they are functioning. Such understanding and insights will undoubtedly improve the quality of care given to clients and patients as their needs are more likely to be adequately assessed and met and their care is more likely to be properly evaluated.

Sociologists commonly attempt to challenge traditions, to explode myths, to debunk irrational behaviour, to expose social inequalities and to document objective facts derived from a continually fostered philosophical and scientific spirit of social enquiry. But, at the same time, sociologists recognise the influences and social functions of tradition, myth, irrationality and ideology. A sociological perspective on health care and nursing should therefore enhance the functions of their practitioners and this book has been written hopefully as a means towards that end.

That the book has appeared at all is due to no small extent to the tenacious and patient encouragement of the publishers and to the meticulous typing skills of my secretary, Mrs Ann Weller. I thank them both.

London, 1976 J.P.S.

Contents

1

The science of sociology

WHAT IS SOCIOLOGY?

Even though men have observed their own societies and groups from early times, sociology is just over a hundred years old. Its chief intellectual antecedents were political philosophy, the philosophy of history, biological theories of evolution and the social and political reform movements of the nineteenth century which triggered off the need for surveys of social conditions.

Sociology was one of the first sciences to be concerned with social life as a whole, that is the complex system of social institutions and social groups. The sociologist's directing idea is that of social structure and he systematically studies aspects of social life such as the family, social stratifications, morals, religion and urban life as well as political and economic institutions.

A concise definition is difficult, but perhaps the best description of sociology is that it is a study of social facts which are ways of acting, feeling and thinking common to a society which coerce individuals in that society to conform. Societal rules cause the individual to conform and he *internalises* the rules as they are taught and acted out by others at all stages of his life so that they become part of his 'outlook on life.' Sociological concepts such as *attitude* and *anomie* enable sociologists to communicate and to converse and exchange meanings with each other and to avoid long wordy exchanges. There is nothing mysterious about the practice: nurses for example often use concepts such as *appendectomy* and *haemoptysis* and *total patient care* for similar reasons.

The study of sociology enables one to look at society in a certain way but, for many novices, developing a sociological perspective takes time. For nursing and other health care students it has dangers in so far as the professional perspective they will want to develop is a nursing (or caring) perspective. There might be a danger of some distortion if an attempt is made to 'fit' the nursing perspective into a sociological perspective.

Nursing science is a unique mix of biological, social and other sciences: in a similar way medicine and engineering are unique mixes of other sciences. The nursing process entails assessing patients needs, planning to meet them, programming the plan and evaluating the programme. Sociology will help towards a better understanding of the differing needs of different individuals with the 'same' medical condition and their different reactions to the 'same' care. The nurse possessing a sociological perspective on care will undoubtedly be in a better position to ensure quality of care to each sick individual in society and be in a better position to function actively in prevention of disease and infirmity.

Sociology claims to be a science of society that sets out to help us to understand, explain and make predictions about members of society. Those who have studied the chemical and physical sciences at school often find sociology's claim to be a science a bit hard to swallow.

WHAT IS A SCIENCE?

So much is implied in the term science. It is commonly used to describe a set of hypotheses that have been subjected to rigorous tests by experiment from which theories of behaviour and activity have been derived on whose strength predictions are made. Making these predictions implies the acceptance of certain explanations of activity based on a cause-effect basis. An important criterion of scientific hypotheses is that there should be a possibility of their refutation, in principle.

The empiricists' or 'pro-naturalistic' view

The physical sciences have a long-standing tradition and prestige as sciences and it is understandable that any new science, like sociology, should attempt to mimic them. Amongst Wundt's generation there was an obvious attempt to copy physics in the reform of *psychology*.

Supporters of the empiricists' or pro-naturalistic view hold that there is no difference in principle between the study of social phenomena and natural phenomena. They assert that methodology is the same throughout the natural and social sciences and although they concede that prediction, e.g. of revolutions, is difficult for the sociologist, it is held that the reason for this is the complexity of the situation. And they also quickly point out that in the physical sciences, for example, no solution is offered to the 'Three Body Problem' by Newtonian mechanics.

Prediction

It is important to distinguish between the behaviour of individuals and the behaviour of groups when considering the aspect of prediction in science. There is, as Lipsey (1963) points out, a 'large number of cases in both the natural and the social sciences in which it is possible to predict with remarkable accuracy how the group will behave without necessarily being able to predict accurately the behaviour of any one member of the group'. No social scientist could predict the particular individuals to be killed on the roads during the next holidays, he points out, but, given the state of the weather on the day and the increase in car sales in the previous year, the closer will the social scientist predict total deaths.

This successful prediction is based on the so called statistical 'law' of large numbers which asserts that random movements of large numbers of individual items tend to cancel each other out. 'This law is based on one of the most beautiful constants of behaviour in the whole of science, natural and social, and yet it can be derived from the fact that human beings make errors!'

The critical thing to notice about a scientific prediction is that it is a *conditional* statement (in both the social and natural sciences) of the form: '*If* you do this *then* such and such will follow', e.g. '*If* you mix hydrogen and oxygen under specified conditions, *then* water will result' and '*If* the government has a large budget deficit, *then* the volume of employment will be increased'.

It must be conceded however that predictions in sociology affect the outcome and there is adequate evidence in the literature of educational research of the possibility of the 'self-fulfilling prophecy' of teachers' predictions of their pupils' attainments.

But the fact that the prediction in social science can be affected by the 'prediction' itself, or not be realised at all because of changed circumstances need not detract from the scientific basis of the prediction. For I could predict that if an apple drops from point X on a tree that it should arrive at point Y on the ground (using the laws of physical science). However if a strong gust of wind blows the apple off course during transit so that it finally arrives at point Z on the ground, it could not be argued that my prediction was 'wrong'. But as Lipsey points out with regards to the 'deficit' and 'rise in employment' example cited above, if the government does have a large deficit and the volume of employment does not rise, a (conditional) scientific prediction has purely been *refuted*. And that is an important element in science.

The experiment

The experimental method is probably the method par excellence of the physical sciences and as Popper (1961) indicates those who oppose the use of the experimental method in the social sciences point out that the very performance of social experiments changes the conditions of society, and artificial isolation for experimental purposes might well eliminate some factors which may be important to the social scientist. And this argument is plausible, for it must be conceded that if 'controls' were used this would tend to be artificial when related to the real world. Indeed it would be rare to find the ideal control situation in any of the social sciences as often one cannot be perfectly clear about what (variable) is being manipulated. For example, in a study of children in a hospital ward, various influences will be impinging on the children at the same time as the 'experiment' is being conducted because of the fact that they are affected by social interaction in a way that could not be claimed in an experiment on 'atoms'. It is also very difficult to clarify whether or not all the children are affected in the same way by the same things. And furthermore, often the social scientist's work is of a qualitative nature and therefore not so precise, insofar as quality is very difficult to measure.

Repetition of social experiments is not possible, it could be argued, because some learning will have taken place as a result of the former experiment. Subsequent experiments will therefore be *new*, not repeats. This makes it difficult to refute hypotheses.

And even if the experimental method were applicable, it could be argued that there is no point in using it as similar conditions only occur within the limits of a single period and the significance of the findings would therefore be limited. But Popper challenges this contention by pointing out that repeats in physical experiments may also be 'new' in that pieces of electric wire used in two so-called 'identical' physical experiments may in fact be different; one may be thicker than the other when it is carefully scrutinised. And the result could be different when the place of the experiment is changed. He also stresses that a piece of apparatus cannot be isolated from all influences as the experimenter does not know *a priori* the influences of the moon or the planets on the experiment. It must be conceded therefore that there appear to be some elements of 'act of faith' in all kinds of experiment—physical or social.

Neither does the doctrine of difference between historical periods make social experiments impossible in Popper's view. It merely expresses the assumption that in another period our piecemeal experiments would teach us, he argues, that certain social conditions would vary in different historical periods!

It is a fact, he holds, that many physical experiments are carried out in undesirable conditions. And, furthermore, astronomers cannot experiment at all!

Popper further argues that Kepler's laws are valid only for the planetary system but not only for the period in which he lived. And Newton did not have to withdraw to another part of the universe for the observation of moving bodies free from the influence of gravity in order to see the importance of the law of inertia, which, although it is of significance in the world, does not lose significance in the solar system.

Furthermore, he asserts, physical atoms also change with the environment in accordance with, not in defiance of, the laws of physics, e.g. by the influence of electro-magnetic fields. And he rightly adds that one can never be sure that even in natural laws there is a law of universal validity, yet it is never asserted that these laws are for a period only. Indeed the best it is possible to do after any experiment is to state that a law or theory is 'consistent with the facts' or 'refuted by the facts' irrespective of the scientific discipline.

If laws subject to change were admitted to, Popper argues, change could never be explained by laws. 'It would be an admission that change is simply miraculous.' And, in his view, this holds for the social sciences no less than for the physicial sciences.

Science is a human progress

That outstanding scientist, J. Bronowski (1964) puts that matter into perspective, in my view, when he asserts that science is not a set of findings but a search for them. 'Science is not a mechanism but a human progress and not a set of findings but the search for them . . . human search and research is a learning by steps of which none is final and the mistakes of one generation are rungs in the ladder, no less than their correction by the next . . . William Blake said that 'to be in error and to be cast out is part of God's design'. It is certainly part of the design of science, he holds. And he adds that there never was a great scientist who did not make bold guesses, and there never was a bold man whose guesses were not sometimes wild.

In the language of science, he asserts, every fact is a field—a criss-cross of implications: those that lead to it and those that lead from it. Truth in science is an ordering of facts. In his view, we organise our experience in patterns, which, when formalised, make the network of scientific laws which are condensed around concepts. So, he argues, science takes its coherence, its intellectual and imaginative strength together, from the concepts at which its laws cross, like knots in a mesh.

It seems to me that if this can be assumed for science, then social science in general and sociology in particular fit well into this framework. And the same can be said for his discussion of verification.

Verification

A question is posed by Bronowski. Can verification (i.e. confirmation) be accepted as a principle if it is assumed to be carried out by one man? Citing Einstein in 1905, he says that Einstein did not debate whether time and space may be absolute, in principle: he asked how physicists in fact measured them. 'So it is irrelevant (and metaphysical) to debate whether verification can be absolute, in principle; the question is, how do men in fact verify a statement?'

'How do they confirm or deny the assertion, for example, that the Crab Nebula is the dust of a supernova which exploded in 1054, and it flows because some of it is radioactive carbon which was made in the supernova?' This is done simply, he contends, by acknowledging that, even in the verification of facts, the help of others who have preceded us as scientists is needed and he further contends that all scientists have to accept this 'principle of truthfulness' for without it individulas would be helpless to tell true from false.

Opponents of the empiricist viewpoint: the concept of 'meaningfulness'

Those who oppose the empiricist viewpoint argue that the keynote phenomena of human behaviour differ essentially from those of inert matter because they have a dimension of 'meaningfulness' which the latter do not. The phenomena of physical sciences, it is held, are 'essentially meaningless' in that the order they display is only a causal regularity. Insofar as they can be said to have significance, it is only a borrowed significance which theories lend them, for human beings endow natural phenomena with meaning which the natural phenomena are unable to do themselves. Therefore it is argued that the phenomena of physical science are different in kind, not merely in degree of complexity from the phenomena of social science. On these premises it is held that any attempt to understand social matters in terms of natural science is 'an unwarranted extrapolation from the history of science'. The analysis of social life involves concepts of purpose and intention, 'concepts which are those in whose terms the agents themselves understand their own behaviour,' as Ryan (1970) puts it.

It is somewhat difficult to reply to this contention and indeed the argument that natural phenomena are endowed with meaning finds some support in Bronowski's comments:

'There is of course no such thing as gravitation sensible to touch. It is neither seen nor heard . . .' Like "mass", it is a creation: symbols which do not exist without the creation by man. 'Solid as it seems, there is no such thing as mass . . .'

'We have grown up with these symbolic concepts, so that we are startled to be told that man had once to create them for himself.' But does it matter? It could be argued with some conviction that the sociologists' concepts such as *alienation, anomie, social distance, attitude, deviance* do not exist without the creation and it certainly could not be said that, for the majority of the members of society, they are terms with which 'the agents themselves understand their own behaviour.' Furthermore, interpretation of the terms often differs even among sociologists and their fellow social scientists!

The concept of meaningfulness is also supported by Winch (as cited by Ryan). In an attempt to detract from support of a causal analysis approach in social science, Winch holds that connections which hold between actions are conceptual connections and the terminology which is employed in talking about actions is indispensable to our identifying actions as actions.

'Human actions, on this view, are meaningful, and meaning is not a category open to causal analysis; thus, so long as meaningful actions form the subject matter of social enquiry, the most important category of our understanding of social life will not be that of cause and effect, but that of meaningfulness and rule-guidedness.'

But conceptual connections can be found in the physical and natural sciences; it could be argued that that is an attribute of all science. For example, Kepler collected data from astronomical observations. Order was found in those data and likeness explored. Later, Newton created the concept of gravity. 'The creation was a concept—a connected set of concepts', Bronowski asserts; 'the concept of a universal gravitation . . . There was (also) the concept of other universal forces in space, which try to pull the moon away. . . . And there was (also) the conept which put an end to the four elements of Aristotle; the concept of mass alike in all earthly and heavenly bodies.'

Putting things into a nutshell, Bronowski adds: 'The concept of gravity was real and true . . . And the concept is tested as we test the man, by its behaviour.' In that respect therefore astronomy and sociology do not differ.

Subjectivity

It could be argued and to some extent conceded that there is a greater problem of subjectivity in the social sciences than in the physical sciences because of understanding and possible empathy of the social scientist. But in conceding subjectivity, surely the social scientist is enhancing his objectivity by actively fostering an awareness of the possible distortion of work and findings by his subjectivity. In any case, no matter what the scientific discipline, there must be some value judgements entailed in the work. For example, the choice of work is normally a personal one; the decision that one has sufficient data is a personal (subjective) decision—as is the decision to follow a suggestion thrown up during investigations and experiments. The need to achieve 'positive' findings may well detract from objective observations in the physical sciences, bound up with the need for prestige resulting from publications. Examples could also be cited of the theoretical framework of the scientist affecting the experimental situation, e.g. Galen's work on the circulation of blood which influenced many future workers for centuries, though his work did not lose stature as scientific (Stevenson, 1964).

Measurement

Physical scientists have developed sophisticated tools of measurement and it could be argued that therein lies the possibility of achieving greater objectivity. But what is this tool of measurement? Nothing more than a tool created by the scientist which may even be distorted by temporary disturbance in perception and minute damage to weights, rules, scales, and the like. Much measurement is in any case based on assumptions of, for example, the perfect straight line, four right angles making a total of 360°; yet the same arguments could be used about these concepts as Bronowski used about gravity and mass. Measurement is purely an heuristic device devised for ease of comparison, created and endowed with meaning by the physical scientists. Therefore it could be argued that the measurements of the physical scientist are no better or no worse than the measurement tools created by the social scientists for their experiments.

Humourless scientism

Berger (1966) sees little relevance in all this debate about social 'science'. He accepts that certain human values are endemic to all scientific (natural and social) procedures, namely:

1. effacement of self in the search for understanding
2. honesty and precision in method
3. respect for findings honestly arrived at
4. patience and willingness to be proved wrong and to revise one's theories, and
5. the community of others sharing these values.

But he urges sociologists not to fixate themselves 'in the attitude of humourless scientism that is blind and deaf to the buffoonery of the social spectacle', lest they find a foolproof methodology, only to lose the world of phenomena that they originally set out to find. He wants social scientists to rid themselves of the grim humourlessness 'invoking terms such as "empirical", "data", "validity" . . . as a voodoo magician might his most cherished hobgoblins'. And he rightly points out that the physical scientists have long since mellowed in their approach to the methods of their science which now allows them to see the methods as relative and limited in scope. But he stresses that the 'scientific' procedures used by sociologists employ specific values, viz.

1. giving careful attention to matters that other scholars might consider pedestrian and unworthy of scientific investigation
2. listening to others without volunteering one's own views, and
3. responsibility for evaluating one's findings, as far as psychologically possible, with regard to one's own prejudices, likes, dislikes, hopes or fears.

It seems to me, however, that he is merely reiterating the history of science; all this could be true to a greater or lesser extent of the other sciences and indeed Berger himself agrees that responsibility for evaluating one's findings 'is shared with other disciplines'.

He would, however, like sociology to be assigned to the vicinity of the humanities as it focuses on 'what it means to be a man and what it means to be a man in a particular situation'. He feels that this will be obscured by the paraphernalia of scientific research and by the bloodless vocabulary developed to legitimate the 'scientific status' of sociology.

But even if one accepts this about sociology then in my view it is very important that what it means to be a man in the present world situation is documented in such a way as to be convincing to the other scientists whose products have great implications for the quality of life, health and care of man in society. Social science could well be the only means of infiltrating the world of the natural and physical scientists with a sense of humanity. The scientific status of sociology is put succinctly by Bottomore (1962) who states that any advances that have been made in sociology are due to the increasing use of the ordinary methods of science:

1. formation of hypotheses, stating a causal connection or correlation, and testing by:
2. collection of data, and
3. analysis of data.

As he points out, the techniques of collection and analysis are becoming increasingly refined. Even though he concedes the difficulty in measuring and subsuming 'under relations of causality', he holds quite rightly that this does not involve a radical difference in methods of enquiry. It merely, in his view, 'involves considering the limits upon sociological enquiry and assessing more realistically what it can achieve'. Comments with which I entirely concur. Methods and intentions are scientific he contends because sociology is concerned with facts, not value judgements upon them. It brings empirical evidence in support of statements made. It is objective because no one is prevented from basing statements upon consideration of the evidence. More rational judgements are therefore made possible.

And even when it is not possible to explain phenomena, reasonable predictions can sometimes be made. Some social phenomena can also be explained under more general statements; but here Bottomore admits serious limitations for, in his view, the generalisations of sociology can only describe trends or tendencies.

Partly in sympathy with and partly admonishing Berger's viewpoint he asserts: 'It is not, as some have supposed, a reliable indication of scientific maturity to use increasingly quantitative methods, but it is a sign of maturity that sociologists are becoming more modest in their claims and more self-critical in evaluating their methods and results'.

NURSING AND SOCIOLOGY

Two other sociologists, both of whom are nurses (Chapman, 1976; Cox, 1979), have clearly demonstrated the ways in which the disciplines of nursing and sociology complement each other. They have illustrated how knowledge and theories from one can help to illuminate and contribute to the other.

As nursing and sociology are both concerned with people and their interactions, Chapman (1976) suggests that it is likely that the theories developed in either the discipline of nursing or in sociology will provide insights for the other. For example, she views the theory of social exchange in the light of the patient and nurse seeking to meet their own needs and goals. She also considers organisation theories and the effects of patterns of compliance and power on achievement of goals. And some tentative explanations are offered for the behaviour of patients or nurses who might be considered deviant.

However, although Chapman attempts to show the relevance of a number of sociological theories to nursing, she concedes that these need testing in the field of nursing to decide their usefulness. She also points out that theories relating to human activity only predict with a variable degree of accuracy because 'although humans as a group may behave similarly, allowance has always to be made for the idiosyncratic'. As nursing falls into the category of human activity, developing nursing theories is therefore fraught with the same problems as sociology and other social and behavioural sciences.

'If that activity called nursing is a mixture of both the behavioural and social sciences it may be permissible', Chapman suggests, 'to borrow concepts from these disciplines in the development of nursing theory. However, their place of origin must not be forgotten'. And that last comment is of profound importance to nurses reading sociology. Cox (1979) suggests that there is even more than a complementary relationship between nursing and sociology and that a 'symbiotic relationship' exists between the two disciplines. She believes that sociology can help nurses achieve their primary objective of good patient care. Sociology, she argues, is particularly relevant to nursing in relation to society's changing patterns of disease, dependency and death, the social and cultural variations in perception of, and responses to disease, analyses of organisations, and interpersonal relationships.

Nursing as the major caring profession is permeated by paradoxes, and has therefore a particular fascination for sociologists. But Cox gives a warning which other sociologists would endorse—that nursing should 'not make itself vulnerable to ideology in the guise of sociology'. 'There is an even greater need to recognise that humility is appropriate and dogmatism is dangerous. If the introduction of sociology to nursing is to be beneficial, I suggest that care must be taken to ensure that it is academically sound: brash ideology and intellectually cheap dogmatism would do more harm than good' (Cox 1979).

REFERENCES

Berger, P.I. (1966) *Invitation to Sociology*. Harmondsworth: Pelican.

Bottomore, T.B. (1962) *Sociology: a Guide to Problems and Literature*. London: Unwin.

Bronowski, J. (1964) *Science and Human Values*. Harmondsworth: Pelican.

Chapman, C.M. (1976) The use of sociological theories and models in nursing. *Journal of Advanced Nursing*, **1**, 111–127.

Cox, C.A. (1979) Who cares? Nursing and sociology: the development of a symbiotic relationship. *Journal of Advanced Nursing*, **4**, 237–252.

Lipsey, R.G. (1963) *An Introduction to Positive Economics.* London: Weidenfield & Nicholson.
Popper, K.R. (1961) *The Poverty of Historicism.* London: Routledge & Kegan Paul.
Stevenson, S.M. (1964) Circulation of the blood: theories since Galen. *Nursing Mirror,* 31 July.
Ryan, A. (1970) *The Philosophy of Social Science.* London: Macmillan.

2

The family's influence
Feeding
Weaning
Moral training
Language development
Love and affection
Sex role-models
The school's influence
Offsetting home deficiencies
Streaming
Alienation
Influences of tradition

Socialisation: becoming an individual in society

Socialisation is the process by which individuals acquire the attitudes, values and practices of the groups they live and work in. Generally the concept of socialisation is applied to the infant (primary socialisation) but increasingly it is applied to the older child entering school and to adults (secondary socialisation) entering professions, work situations or deviant settings. In fact, socialisation is an ongoing process that continues throughout life for everyone.

The socialisation of the infant is brought about primarily by parents controlling his behaviour until he conforms to and *internalises* their attitudes and expectations of how a child should behave with the implicit aim of ensuring that he will become a socially adequate adult member of society. This is based, of course, on the assumption that their own attitudes and expectations are right and appropriate for survival in the society at large.

If the socialisation process proceeds satisfactorily the infant will eventually be able to function within normal limits in most of the roles he is required to perform during his lifetime, such as boy, pupil, husband, friend, lawyer. The socialisation process is not always a smooth process but for most people the rough passages are conquered without too much trauma or difficulty. However, threshold levels to trauma and difficulty tend to differ in different individuals and sometimes two individuals who have been exposed to the 'same' socialisation processes turn out to be significantly different kinds of people.

THE FAMILY'S INFLUENCE

The new-born infant is completely dependent on the already functioning world into which he is born, and what he will do, eat, wear, think and believe in the future is intimately related to the kind of family into which he is born.

It must be stressed from the outset however that the human infant should not be considered merely to be a completely malleable lump of protoplasm to be shaped according to a predetermined design. The human infant, dependent as he is on others, does not necessarily take everything as it comes. He can act back and he can reject certain stimuli and seek others instead.

Suggestions of how British infants are socialised have been made by John and Elizabeth Newson (1965) following a study of child-rearing practices in Nottingham.

Even before the birth of the infant, the 'environment' for the working-class and middle-class offspring appears to be significantly different:

'All the evidence suggests, that middle-class mothers tend to become pregnant in happier, or at least more socially acceptable circumstances; that they enter the experience of motherhood with more "enlightened" attitudes; and that they are likely to be more adequately prepared for the adjustments which the arrival of any new baby inevitably demands'.

The study documents a number of interesting features about infant socialisation and also explores certain myths about child rearing practices.

Feeding

Breast feeding of children has declined and this decline in breast feeding is predominantly a working-class phenomenon due to the fact that middle-class wives appear to be strongly influenced by what they perceive to be the demands of 'duty' and 'principle'.

This may be due to a number of factors. Working-class mothers are often embarrassed about breast feeding infants in front of their husbands and other children 'which is probably only one aspect of that general prudishness about nudity which has been noticed by observers', the Newsons add. The working-class mother often feels the need for privacy which tends to be lacking in her home. But she also realises that she can save a fair amount of time by propping up a bottle for her infant and unlike the 'more psychology-conscious middle-class mother, does not consider this as a possible cause of emotional deprivation for her child'. There are clear-cut and consistent class differences in the methods of feeding and in both the incidence and duration of breast feeding shows a definite increase as the scale of social class groupings is ascended. This appears to reflect and perpetuate the typical attitude of working-class mothers that material obligations to one's children are more important than psychological attitudes.

'The working-class mothers feel free to suit themselves in the matter of infant feeding; and often as a result, they are completely out of sympathy with the advice pressed upon them by middle-class nurses and doctors . . .'

Crow (1977) found that mothers tended to be muddled about 'demand feeding' and that those who were breast feeding their infants were probably overemphasising the psychological aspects of the feeding environment. If Auerbach (1979) is right, this muddle reflects the nurse's muddled knowledge on the topic. Although, she argues, the nurse's role in support of breast feeding is crucial, she often receives only sketchy information about how to help mothers who need advice.

Mothers who do not continue breast feeding their infants—and the proportion is higher in women of the lower social classes—also run the risk of affecting the quality of their own lives. In a study conducted in Cambridge, Whichelow (1979) found that sustained lactation benefits the mother: those who were still breast feeding their child three months after birth were less likely to suffer from depression or fatigue.

Weaning

Weaning of infants takes place in two stages, when the breast is first exchanged for the bottle and when the bottle is given up altogether.

Once a baby has become used to a bottle, weaning tends to take longer, and most babies derive a great deal of pleasure from sucking bottles which, the Newsons found, they often demand even as they get older. And this demand is easily satisfied by the not too-determined mother. Moreover, the bottle of warm milk is often used as a soporific to ensure restful nights for the parents. This inevitably prolongs the sucking period and prevails in most working-class homes and fifty per cent of the middle-class homes as well. But mothers who allow bottle-sucking well into the second or third year 'are more likely to be working class', as are mothers who assume that dummies are a normal part of a baby's sucking equipment.

'The working-class child, more often denied the close personal relationship of prolonged breast feeding, has as compensation a very long period of bottle feeding to look forward to, with the additional comfort of the dummy, usually available at any time.'

Moral training

Even in the baby's first few months of life, his behaviour is often evaluated in moral terms: 'easy, passive babies are held as models of perfection and natural goodness'.

There is some indication that parents of different social classes attach importance to different aspects of what is considered 'naughty' and to different aspects of child training.

Middle-class women appear to have a deep-seated objection to allowing a child to continue with the infantile practice of sucking for mere pleasure during the second year of life in comparison with working-class women. The middle-class mother also starts the process of weaning from bottle to dummy earlier. 'As the child nears his first birthday . . . if the dummy has been allowed at all, she will be setting limits to that "bad habit" . . .'

'Good' sleeping habits are developed from early days in middle-class children. They have a greater tendency than working-class children to have a normal bedtime before 6:30 pm and are more likely to have a room of their own. Discipline and independence are therefore attitudes which are fostered from early days in middle-class homes.

There are also clear and very marked class differences in attitudes towards masturbation in children. 'Nearly all of class V mothers try to stop the child touching or playing with his genitals . . . only a quarter of professional men's wives do . . . this squeamishness about the exposure of the body appears as an exclusively working-class feeling.' This working-class 'modesty' is apparent, as noted above, in breast feeding, and also in toilet training practices of working-class mothers.

An analysis of the Newsons' study suggests that on the whole the working-class family fosters permissiveness and immediate gratification of need in its socialisation of infants with regard to the methods of feeding, weaning and toilet training, whereas the middle-class family ethos is one that fosters self-discipline and independence. It could be argued therefore that as to achieve anything in life entails a fair amount of self-discipline in that one must often forego immediate gratification for long term benefits, the middle-class infants' better life chances are enhanced from the days of primary socialisation. Because of the values he internalises he may be more likely to extend his education past minimum school leaving age, giving up the chances of earning a wage at sixteen (immediate gratification) so that he can improve his long-term earning potential after a period of higher education, as in fact is usually the case.

The study also indicates how certain attitudes to 'right', 'good' and 'moral' behaviour are laid down in very early days of life—and hence they are particularly difficult to change.

Language development

One of man's most important faculties is language and the ability to verbalise communications. Where language development is defective, communication will be impaired and it will also have some negative effects on educational attainment. In a study of language development in Aberdeen, Nisbett (1967) demonstrates the close association between having a low intelligence quotient (IQ) as measured by conventional intelligence tests, which were commonly used in selection processes, and being a member of a large family. As IQ tests depend to a very great extent on the language ability of the children taking them the study, not surprisingly, further indicates the low IQ scores were closely associated with inadequate language development in children from large families. An analysis of the findings of the study suggests that the reason for children from large families being at a disadvantage is because the mothers, being overworked and harassed, have too little time for contact with their children and as a result the children are unable to master the 'mother-tongue'. In these families, it is hypothesised, language is learned from older siblings and therefore undeveloped and unsophisticated language skills are learned. On the other hand, in a small family mother has time to give attention to and play with her children and to give them more personal attention and to communicate directly with them. Children from these families therefore develop better language skills. As family size tends to increase from social class I to V, it follows that the children of working-class parents are more likely to develop defective language skills and suffer the inevitable consequences in later life of poor educational attainment.

Another thesis, postulated by Bernstein (1965), places emphasis on changes in the social structure as major factors in shaping or changing a given culture through their effect on the consequences of fashions of speaking. As the child learns his speech, he argues, he learns the requirements of his social structure. Two *codes* of speech are identified: a 'restricted' code and an 'elaborated' code. The restricted code is the kind of speech pattern used by everyone in the company of relatives and intimate friends and requires a minimum of words; more is often communicated by nods, movements of hands and facial expressions than by actual verbalisation. The elaborated code, however, entails a greater degree of verbalisation and a more sophisticated sentence construction and he holds that this code must be well developed for conceptual thinking to be possible. This ability to conceptualise is considered essential for progress through centres of higher education.

As the working-class child appears generally to be exposed only to the restricted code at home he is at a distinct disadvantage to the middle-class child who is exposed to both codes and who can therefore fluctuate between the two codes according to the situation. This obviously gives him a social advantage in that he can communicate adequately with all sections but, at school, he has a distinct advantage:

'Where a child is sensitive to an elaborated code the school experience . . . is one of symbolic and social development; for the child limited to a restricted code the school is one of symbolic and social change'.

Love and affection

Love cannot be studied in families in the same way that feeding and weaning behaviour can; neither can it be studied in humans in a laboratory. Much of the 'knowledge' available on the effects of care, or lack of it, on humans has been derived from clinical studies, conducted by staff of the Tavistock Clinic, London; but generalising about what is normal from a study of the abnormal is fraught with difficulties. Indeed the Tavistock maternal deprivation thesis that children deprived of maternal love become socially deprived adults has been eruditely discussed for many years since the 1950s by, among others, Bowlby and Fry (1953) and I think, at last, it might be possible to accept that a sense of perspective has now been achieved in the consensus view that it is the quality of love and not the quantity that is significant.

Margaret and Harry Harlow (1965), following a study of primates in laboratory situations, suggest that love or affection is not a single emotion or single function but that there are at least five basic affectional or love systems 'and each of these follows an orderly growth or developmental pattern; each is called forth by its own appropriate set of stimulus conditions'.

The five systems are: the infant affectional system—the love of the infant for its mother; the maternal affectional system—the love of the mother for her infant; the age-mate affectional system—the affection of infants and children for each other within and between the sexes; the hetero- or alterosexual affectional system—the passionate love between adolescent and adult men and women; and finally, the paternal affectional system—the love of the adult male for younger members of his social group

For normal emotional and social development to occur the Harlows' work suggests that 'intimate bodily contact' of the infant with mother, play between mother and child and opportunities for play between growing children are essential.

'The patterns of play become progressively more complex and progressively more social. They start as individual play or play with mother. They change into increasingly complex patterns of age-mate interaction, and they train the child in the problems and perplexities of knowing, adjusting to, and accepting the social roles he will enjoy with the generation to which he belongs. Some will learn leadership, and others will learn to follow.'

The Newsons' study suggests significant class differences in bodily contact in terms of breast feeding between infant and mother. Nisbett's work indicates that the mother of the large (usually working-class) family has little time to give much individual attention to her children; she is therefore not very likely to have much time for play. Does this not suggest that there might well be significant class differences in opportunities for adequate and social development in children of different social classes? The implications are serious, for although the Harlows concede that 'monkeys will never be men', they hold that 'the basic forms of love or affection are deep and abiding mechanisms'. This is supported in their work which indicates that, among other findings, none of the partially socially deprived male monkeys had ever made an adequate sexual adjustment. All of the socially deprived female monkeys that became mothers were inadequate mothers to their first babies. All the babies would have died if the Harlows had not intervened and fed them. 'What is more, all the deprived mothers abused their babies, and three babies out of the first ten were killed by their mothers, or died of injuries shortly after we separated them.' The aetiology of the battered baby syndrome seems to start in early socialisation.

'Hunger, thirst, danger, and even sexual needs come and go', the Harlows argue, 'but the orderly operation of social unity continues unaffected, supported and maintained by the deep and unending affectional bonds . . .'

Sex role-models

It seems generally true, the Newsons argue, that in British society as one proceeds down the social scale the sex roles become more sharply defined and more rigidly typed. In the socially lower classes there are clear distinctions between 'men's work' and 'women's work' and 'as we move from white-collar to manual occupations, the father's work is more likely to consist of some activity outside the wife's own range of experience'.

In the family, these general social class differences find expression in the role the wife casts her husband.

A working-class man's wife feels called upon to minister to his 'physical needs as a matter of first priority . . . Her first function is to feed him'. She also has to accept that his social life is dominated by 'exclusively male companionship'.

The middle-class man's wife's efforts are 'likely to be directed less towards the husband himself than towards the home as his setting. . .', so that she can prove to be his 'social asset'.

The role of 'mummy' appears to be accepted with dissatisfaction by middle-class wives, particularly the better-than-average educated, whereas the role of 'mum' has high status for the working-class wife.

Both types of wives' roles are obviously passive and differ

significantly from the apparent dominant gregarious roles of the middle- and working-class fathers on whom they are dependent. These are the male and female role-models with which the developing children, boy and girl, obviously identify.

Clearly, the family's influence on the socialisation of the child is not only significant but also multi-factorial.

THE SCHOOL'S INFLUENCE

The potential of the school as a socialising agent should not be underestimated as some of the early pioneers of educational reform have demonstrated in their philosophies.

The British public school system grew as a result of nineteenth century legislation making entry examinations to the church, law and army compulsory. This spurred on the social elite to provide an education for their sons which would guarantee that the previously perceived-to-be 'born' leaders could in future be 'made' into leaders.

Mathew Arnold's principles at Rugby were merely mirroring the age in which he lived. He knew that servants were commonly employed by 'gentlemen' and, believing therefore that it would be useful for his public school pupils to know what it felt like to be a servant, introduced the fagging system in which younger pupils acted as servants to the older boys (Peterson 1960).

The socialisation possibilities in education are even discernible in Plato's *Republic*: he suggests that whereas for the philosopher king the aim of education is the vision of the 'Good', for the ordinary man it is 'that schooling from boyhood in goodness which inspires the recipient with passionate and ardent desire to become a perfect citizen'.

Its potential has been perceived and engineered in the 20th century. When Hitler came to power in Germany in the 1930s, he promptly and very efficiently linked the German education system to his own social and political ends, viz. glorification of the German race, complete obedience to the Fuhrer and the creation of healthy and vigorous bodies. An analysis of the American system indicates that it is attempting to produce 'little' Americans, which is probably an essential aspect of education in such a multi-immigrant society. American children study a great deal about American society and literature, national heroes are held up to be paragons of virtue and teachers constantly look back on the origins of the state to inculcate national values. Allegiance to the state is fostered daily by the tribute paid to the American flag.

Indeed it could be argued that the recommendations of the Education Act of 1944 merely reflect the national self-consciousness produced during wartime and the consequent desire to bring British society nearer to the ideal of an egalitarian society. Rab Butler, in commenting on the 1944 Act in the first Noel Buxton Lecture delivered at the University of Essex, indicates that the Act made religious instruction the only compulsory subject in the British secondary school curriculum because it epresented the pervading ethos of the country and the 'right' values for its citizens which appears to be explicitly conceding and exploiting the school's contribution to socialisation. This fact is also reflected in the Scottish Report on secondary education published in 1947 which states: 'What is the aim of education is a question that admits of no answer without a reference to ultimate convictions about human nature and destiny about society and how the individual stands related to it'.

It is not the prime purpose of this text to demonstrate that a nation's educational system is its philosophy in practice but to indicate that consideration of underlying philosophies can sometimes put a sociological discussion in a more meaningful perspective.

That being said it is now appropriate to return to a consideration of some relevant sociological studies.

Offsetting home deficiencies

A large-scale study of individuals from birth to the age of 21 carried out by Douglas (1964) showed that very good schools may offset the deficits derived from poor and non-supportive homes, provided that these are not too extreme. He also shows that very bad schools produce negative effects of varying severity.

Streaming

Other work documented by Jackson for the Crowther Committee, and by Hargreaves (1967), demonstrates the effects of streaming of schoolchildren which is usually reinforcing the social class position of the child in that the lower streams tend to consist primarily of children from lower socio-economic families and vice versa. But what is more concerning is that the studies suggest that once a pupil has been labelled according to the stream to which he is allocated, irrespective of his potential ability, he tends to perform academically according to the 'label' of his stream as a self-fulfilling prophecy phenomenon. The work by Jackson shows how the British education system of streaming created an education system in miniature and 'shows how savagely and sadly a school system can become a tenacious self-fulfilling prophecy, cutting talent down in the hunt for the chosen few' (*The Crowther Report* 1959).

Hargreaves' study sets out to examine the basic social processes in a secondary school at 'Lumley' where boys were placed in four streams. Generally, he finds that the higher the stream the greater the commitment demonstrated by the boys to the school's (middle-class) values. The boys also tend to be more satisfied with the school and conform to their teacher's expectations of them. The reverse is true of the boys in the lower streams.

Of the boys in the lowest (D) stream who are perceived by the teachers to be the 'bad' boys, fifty per cent appeared in court at least once and freely admitted to larceny. This compares very unfavourably with the non-delinquent behaviour found in the higher streams. Being placed in the D stream also appears to have affected the boys' social aspirations. They leave school earlier and few make any attempt to find work. The higher the stream, the more time boys spend at home, the more time they spend on homework, the more they belong to organised youth clubs and so on. In Hargreaves' view this suggests that boys placed in high streams are more likely to develop the skills and internalise the values necessary for success in present-day society. He concedes, however, that although 'the extremes can be clearly distinguished, there remains a large proportion of boys who, whilst tending towards one of the poles, cannot easily be contained in either'. In different circumstances, he argues, sub-cultural developments such as demonstrated in the 'academic' and 'delinquent' streams may not take place at all. However, if his findings are valid for other schools then they indicate that the social system of the school (and the teachers) are of fundamental importance in the socialisation process of children.

Alienation

In tracing the subsequent careers and life styles of working-class children who received a grammer school education, Jackson and Marsden (1966) show further how the school's influence on socialisation is potentially powerful insofar as the majority of the children eventually become middle-class adults, having internalised typical middle-class values. Their new social class position had, in many instances, alienated them from their working-class families and friends. 'Grammar school brought them into an alien world' but even the 'early leavers' who left school before completion of official examinations 'like many working-class boys and girls who had been unsuccessful at a higher stage of education, they *knew* this . . . They rejected the values of Huddersfield's business class above them, and were unable to merge again into working-class life'. They became social misfits.

An international study conducted by the International Association of Evaluation of International Achievement (IEA) in Hechinger's analysis (1973) shows that open access to public education is a key factor in allowing lower socio-economic class children to rise to the level of the 'academic élite' which increases their chances of economic success. Furthermore, it demonstrates that it is 'actually the selective system that pays a price in lost talent and social dislocation'. In the highly selective German schools, for example, only one per cent of 18-year-old students were from lower-class homes compared with 14 per cent in the non-selective American schools.

It could be argued therefore that open access to a school system does much to break down the concept of a class-based society.

Influences of tradition

In considering the school influences and those of the family on the infant and child, the influence of tradition in different areas of the country might be quite important and should not be excluded from the discussion, as indicated from time to time in comments by education reports such as those of David Fletcher (1975) of *The Daily Telegraph* who in investigating the reasons why Welsh children head the country's list of brainiest pupils suggests that this is because there is a 'tradition of study among children' in Wales. 'They do not have the attraction of high salaries at an early age, so they stay on at school . . .' And Pearce Wright (1969), commenting in *The Times* on a study of 11 000 seven year olds which suggested that the happiest children were in Scotland, finds that traditionally a greater proportion of Scottish parents are interested in their children's schooling and progress and that Scottish parents tend to spend more time with their children.

Socialisation is obviously the outcome of the interplay of a large number of factors.

Children adopt the values of their parents and adolescents those of their peers and adult role models. Social class remains a most powerful influence throughout life. 'An abiding impression must be of the very substantial extent of the differences between the middle (non-manual) and the working (manual) classes, and the stark differences between the extremes: the professional and the unskilled manual classes' (Reid, 1977).

REFERENCES

Auerbach, K.G. (1979) The role of the nurse in support of breast feeding. *Journal of Advanced Nursing,* **4,** 236–285.

Bernstein, B. (1965) A socio-linguistic approach to learning in *Penguin Survey of the Social Sciences* ed. by Gould, J.

Bowlby, J. & Fry, M. (1953) *Child Care and the Growsth of Love*. Harmonsworth: Pelican.

Crow, R.A. (1977) An etnological study of the development of infant feeding. *Journal of Advanced Nursing* **2,** 99–109.

Douglas, J.W.B. (1964) *The Home and the School*. London: MacFibbon & Kee.

Fletcher, D. (1975) Welsh children head country's list of brainiest children. *The Daily Telegraph*, 8th April.

Harlow, M.K. & H.F. (1965) An anlysis of love. *The Listener*, 18th February.

Hechinger, F.M. (1973) Pupil performance: home is a crucial factor. *The New York Times*, 27th May.

Jackson, B. & Marsden, D. (1966) *Education and the Working Class*. Pelican.

Newson, J. & E. (1965) *Patterns of Infant Care in an Urban Community*. Pelican.

Nisbett, J. (1967) Family environment and intelligence (in *Education. Economy and Society* edited by A.H. Halsey *et al*. London: Collier-Macmillan.

Peterson, A.D.C. (1960) *A Hundred Years of Education*. New York: Collier Books.

Reid, I. (1977) *Social Class Differences in Britain: a Source Book*. London: Open Books.

Whichelow, M.J. (1979) Breast feeding in Cambridge, England: factors affecting the mother's milk supply. *Journal of Advanced Nursing,* **4,** 253–261.

Wright, P. (1969) Happiest children are in Scotland. *The Times*, 10th September.

Life chances
Social class influences
Dangers of overgeneralisation
Health life chances
Mental and physical disorders
Women's lot in society
Deviancy
Cultural influences
Application to nursing

3

Implications of socialisation

An interest in the implications of socialisation for the individual in society can be detected in the writings of a number of sociologists some of which are briefly discussed below.

Durkheim in his study of the division of labour in society polarises society into two types which he calls *mechanical solidarity and organic solidarity*. In mechanical solidarity society, people are mentally and morally homogeneous and their communities are uniform. Their society is characterised by a *collective conscience* which consists of a set of common beliefs and sentiments. But organic solidarity society, he postulates, is atomised and held together by the interpendence of its parts. The division of labour results from the struggle for existence and this stimulates individualism and differentialism.

People in organic solidarity society are heterogeneous and as a consequence the collective conscience, he holds, is weakened and they are therefore mentally and morally dissimilar. This thesis was developed further by Durkheim in his investigation of suicide wherein his emphasis on the strong predominance of the collective conscience in the mechanical solidarity society and the weakening of the collective conscience in the organic solidarity society is supplanted by his recognition of a collective conscience in the organic solidarity society as the basis of either *egositic* or *altruistic* order. In his study of suicide a more specific definition of the absence of the collective conscience is arrived at which he calls *anomic* society in which social action is regulated only on the basis of a shifting and precarious consensus. Society in a state of anomie, he holds, no longer persists in collective beliefs and sentiments.

Social influence on the individual is powerful in his view, and he contends that it is 'a real illusion which makes us believe that personality was so much more complete when the division of labour had penetrated less. No doubt, in looking from without at the diversity of occupations which the individual then embraces, it may seem that he is developing in a very free and complete manner. But, in reality, this activity is not his, it is society, it is the race acting in and through him . . .'.

Cooley (1909) in his observations on social organisation perceives the importance of mutual interaction between the group and the individual and maintains that neither the group nor the individual has primacy in social action. This contrasts with Durkheim's view which gives, as noted above, primacy to the group over the individual. Cooley postulates the concept of the *looking-glass self* and holds that 'self and society are twin born'.

Weber (1947) types social action in terms of rational orientation to a system of discrete individual ends. This is achieved, in his view, through the expectations of individuals as to the behaviour of some objects in the external situation and expectations as to the behaviour of other individuals.

There are, he holds, certain basic elements inherent in all stratified societies. The stratified system must be thought of as containing a number of hierarchies which differ with each variation and combination of the basic stratification factors of *status, class* and *authority*. He concedes that discrepancies in *life chances* may be caused in every society by social mobility among the different positions one person may hold in each of these hierarchies.

The work of Karl Marx, written in nineteenth century England, is preoccupied with the implications for the individual living in a class-based society and the inevitability of *alienation* and growth of *class consciousness* as outcomes of the class struggle in society:

'Owing to the extensive use of machinery and to division of labour, the work of the proletarian has lost all individual character. . . . He becomes an appendage of the machine. . . .'

'. . . The division of labour offers us the first example of how, as long as man remains in natural society, that is as long as a cleavage exists between the particular and the common interest, as long therefore as activity is not voluntarily but naturally divided, man's own deed becomes as alien power opposed to him, which enslaves him instead of being controlled by him. . . .'

The influence of Marx's views is discernible in those of Tonnies, but Tonnies takes a much less deterministic stand and recognises the power of ideas and religious beliefs in society.

In his discussion of *custom* he postulates the concept of *social will* and in his own, albeit rambling, way makes a contribution to the concept of socialisation. For him the word custom designates an actual way of conduct (a *fact*), a general prescription or prohibitive rule of conduct (a *norm*), and, a *will* in the sense that it is often contended that 'custom demands that . . .' (Tonnies, 1951).

In Tonnies' view, social action is interaction guided by general rules which are binding in different degrees but nevertheless demand respect and compliance. His comments on woman are most perceptive:

'Often custom works much the more in favour of the woman the less rights are granted her. In England, up to 100 years ago, the woman was almost completely without rights and even so, England was regarded as the "paradise of women" . . . We are still replete with customs which are brutal. But custom, according to its predominant direction, has a humane character'.

He maintains that the sociologist must in the first instance study and isolate custom as a highly important form of *social will* and that one must perceive and analyse social will similarly to one's perception and analysis of the individual will. 'The same meaning which "will" in the ordinary individual sense has for individual men, "social will" has for every community or society'.

Sorokin (1964) considers and evaluates relative contributions of innate individual differences and environmental differences in the context of postulated concepts of *social space, social distance* and *social position* and makes a number of conclusions, *inter alia*, that there are permanent and fundamental causes of social stratification, which under conditions of living together, permanently operate in the way of creating social stratification.

The causes in his view are innate differences of individuals and differences in environment. And he contends that they are 'quite sufficient to produce all the principal forms of social stratification'.

'As it is improbable that in the future the innate qualities of individuals or their environment will be identical, a complete abolition of social stratification is improbable', he concludes.

Students of socialisation sometimes become concerned at its apparent deterministic implications but they should be assured—and reminded—that the concept of socialisation is, like all concepts are, merely a simple way of observing the complexities of society. Man is not merely a mouldable mass of clay.

In further reassurance, it should be stressed that socialisation has the very functional aspect of enabling the individual to live, work, play and survive in society, summarised so succinctly by Goffman (1969):

'In order to prevent the occurrence of incidents and the embarrassment consequent upon them, it will be necessary for all the participants in the interaction, as well as those who do not participate, to process certain attributes and to express these attributes in practices of saving the show. These attributes . . . the defensive measures used by performers to save their own show; the protective measures used by audience and outsiders to assist the performers in saving the performers' show; and, finally the measures the performers must take in order to make it possible for the audience and outsiders to employ protective measures on the performer's behalf'.

LIFE CHANCES

There is a great deal of evidence to suggest that an individual's social, educational, economic and health life chances, are very closely associated with his social class background and indeed studies of life chances of various social groups, particularly the poorer social classes, have fascinated sociologists for many decades, as Titmuss (1964) points out with feeling:

'When we turn from trying to understand the behaviour of the top income group to studying those at the bottom we find more light if not more sweetness. The poor have for long rendered great service to the behavioural sciences; they have helped to train countless sociologists, doctors and market researchers . . ..'

He goes on to stress that as epidemiological research into disease causation has demonstrated the importance of considering the whole complex of needs, opportunities and resources, the same is true when considering social and economic equality. 'We thus delude ourselves if we think that we can equalise the social distribution of life chances by expanding educational opportunities while millions of children live in slums without baths . . . room to explore and space to learn . . ..'

Differences in cash earnings between different social classes, he claims, have widened substantially 'when calculated over the whole of a man's working life' as the whole system of incremental awards for the professional man is fundamentally different from the pay system traditionally used for manual workers who normally receive no annual increments after being awarded a 'man's wage'. He concedes however that today's working-class youth in the 16–20 age group is better off than his counterpart of the 1930s but points out that they pay more in taxes and social benefit charges than their middle-class contemporaries who continue to be subsidised by the community whilst continuing with-full time higher education. Even though in later life the middle-class youth 'may be twenty times or more better off . . . with less disabling disease, a longer expection of life, a lower age of retirement, more inherited wealth', and 'a more assured pension'.

Titmuss's statement, cited above, about 'disabling disease' finds much support in the conclusions of a *Report on the Work of the Employment Medical Advisory Service* (1975). The report details the diseases peculiar to cable-making, cotton and pottery workers and the effects of working in industries that require continual exposure to asbestos, lead and vinyl chloride.

Rapidly developing technology may create new health hazards, the report warns, and at a speed which challenges the ability to monitor them. The report also calls for new measures to detect hitherto hidden effects of potentially hazardous working conditions. It also indicates that the significance of occupational medicine is, regrettably, still not fully appreciated, even by doctors.

SOCIAL CLASS INFLUENCES

Data obtained from cross-culture comparative studies collected by Lipset and Bendix (1959) confirms that children of families with high social class status have much better life chances than do children of working-class families. But, they contend, it is important to bear in mind that significant minorities of children depart from the typical pattern of their class. Many children with 'favourable family background leave school at an early age, while a considerable number of workers' children manage to continue in school despite obstacles'. This variation of educational attainment within classes, they suggest, indicates that one's family background plays 'an enabling and motivating rather than a determining role'.

They do find, however, that in spite of the fact that relatively large numbers of sons of manual workers complete 'high school' courses, their chances of holding a non-manual position are considerably less than the chances of children of middle-class families with the same education.

If an individual comes from a working-class family, they indicate that he will typically receive little education or vocational advice. This thesis is also supported by Douglas (1964). The working-class child at school has less job plans for the future and when he leaves school he will be vague and tend to take the first available job he can find, a view finding support in the study of Carter (1966) of school leavers entering working life.

Furthermore, Lipset and Bendix find that 'the poverty, lack of education, absence of personal "contacts", lack of planning, and failure to explore fully the available job opportunities that characterise the working-class family are handed down from generation to generation . . . occupation and social status are to an important extent self-perpetuating'.

They further conclude that the inclination to defer immediate gratifications is usually inculcated in middle-class families who tend to combine earlier training for independence with the stronger development of 'self-control' to defer gratifications. Certainly the findings of the Newsons (1965) support this view. This inclination to defer gratification, Bendix and Lipset hold, 'probably contributes to the advantage which the offspring of the middle class have over those from the lower classes'. The potential influence of the family is no less diminished by their statement that the 'childhood experiences of lower-status men who later become business leaders often show a pattern of strong mothers and weak fathers, and an emotionally unsatisfactory life'.

The Plowden Report (*Children and Their Primary Schools,* 1967) demonstrated the influences of the British family on educational attainment of children. The influence of parental attitudes were found to be of great importance and were more positive in middle-class homes. A larger proportion of children with poor maternal care in early childhood were in the lower streams of primary schools than would have been expected from their performance on objective tests and these children in the lower streams tended to get less effective, less experienced teachers and less good facilities than other children. Their educational deprivations were therefore cumulative.

However, there are working-class children who despite the odds against them do reach a level of successful educational attainment. The mark of working-class parents who have successful children, Swift (1967) suggests, is that they have 'longer ideal and practical social horizons than working-class parents of children who do not succeed. They seem to have a clear picture of middle-class life and it is this that forms the foundation for educational success'.

Early selection of pupils which is part of the organisational frame work of secondary modern schools (streaming) encourages the separation of the élite pupils from the average and below average Maddock (1967) contends. At the time of selection, he holds, 'the majority are assigned to an education of relatively low prestige' and argues that this may involve a lowering of self-image. With obvious cynicism he concludes that this early selection of pupils will foster lowered aspirations which will do much to avoid raising hopes and the emergency of discontented leaders to challenge the established social élite.

'It is thought that this process of socialisation into the occupational hierarchy inherent in the organisational framework of our educational system, does more than mould aspirations to a "station in life" . . . It also creates, he holds, an 'academic' and 'practical' orientation to learning. He holds that social class influences on learning are cumulative.

The cumulative effects of social class influence are further noted by Downes and Fowler (1967) who cite a number of studies conducted among secondary modern school boys whose contemporaries were 'selected' for grammer schools. Fifty-five per cent had had no education since leaving school at 15; 26 per cent had experience of day release education. The bulk of these students work for ordinary (ONC) and higher (HNC) national certificates but the failure rate for ONC is 75 per cent and only about 0.9 per cent of those embarking on ONC finally achieve HNC standard.

The small and medium-sized firms which are notoriously inefficient in training apprentices and in granting day release study facilities appear to attract a 'disproportionate' supply of young entrants. Those boys who have already obtained selective (grammar school) education are more likely to receive better and more favourable training opportunities.

Furthermore, Downes and Fowler indicate that 'although the vast majority of secondary modern boys who enter industry via the smaller firm eventually move to the large firm . . . they do so in general only after they have outgrown the age at which the training opportunities of the large firm would have been available to them'.

It is a fact, however, that since the 1960s due to social and political pressures, and in an attempt to enhance the possibility of better educational opportunities for the socially deprived, there has been a reduction in the numbers of selective secondary schools and a massive increase in the numbers of non-selective secondary (comprehensive) schools. The evidence of their effectiveness in meeting objectives is as yet not quite conclusive but there is some evidence to suggest that another deprived group is being created as a result of comprehensive school organisation, namely the 'gifted' child. A report prepared by Sir Cyril Burt (1975) following a special study of the ablest children (with an IQ of 140 or more) in a group of comprehensive schools claims that these children's educational progress and development are being hampered by the teaching methods in comprehensive schools. More than half of the children complained that the school curriculum makes no provision for subjects such as higher mathematics, nuclear physics and molecular biology. A large number protested at the way teachers played down to the less able children. The gifted children's commonest complaint, however, is that they are brighter than their teachers and are able to solve problems more quickly than them.

Home influences are (once more) also detected and the 'child who suffers most is the bright one from the humbler ranks' but children of 'professional people often enjoy the requisite facilities and encouragement at home'.

'Children with parents of mediocre ability and no intellectual interest are doubly handicapped. Nowhere, at home or at school, are they given the opportunities, or the materials, to develop intellectual interests'.

The 'moral', Burt contends, is that a policy of greater diversity in educational organisation should be aimed at instead of the present policy of greater uniformity and he pleads for special residential schools exclusively for these 'gifted' children. His study in some ways echoes the feelings lucidly expressed by a number of academics and edited by Cox and Dyson (1969) in the form of a 'Black Paper' which argues that 'disastrous mistakes are being made in modern education and that an urgent reappraisal is required'. They also warn against possible levelling-down effects of 'the ideology of egalitarianism'.

With some concern Shaw (1969) notes that the authors of the Black Paper have 'nothing to say about adult education' which he holds is 'essentially a process of levelling up' and a way of bridging cultural gaps. He sees great hope in that respect for the effects of the Open University courses.

But even in the 1970s Marsden (1974) still finds that educational inequalities of opportunity persist. The local education authorities' 'league' tables of the 1970s, ranked according to the proportions of their pupils who are sixth formers and who gain university places can still be predicted, he points out, from 'the occupational composition of the area, *regardless of the school system*'. He also finds an overall imbalance in educational spending throughout the country and claims that as less seems to be spent in the educationally deprived areas of the country, such as the north and the east, 'society discriminates against the poor'.

Dangers of overgeneralisation

We should guard against overgeneralisation. As Lipset and Bendix (1959) point out, it cannot be assumed that a higher rate of social mobility necessarily leads to more satisfaction in life for the individual or that a low rate of social mobility leads to discontent. Nor does 'success' through high mobility necessarily result in total—or any—satisfaction as often it creates higher aspirations and a formulated hatred for one's social position and alienation from the family of origin, as Jackson and Marsden's (1966) findings show.

Studies of mental illness in America cited by Lipset and Bendix show that people moving up the social ladder are more likely to have mental breakdowns than the non-mobile. It is probable, they contend, that a particular type of ego structure which results from a characteristic family environment is both favourable for upward mobility and vulnerable to mental illness. Citing data drawn from studies of social class IV and V workers, they further indicate that the upwardly mobile who originate in social class V are more unhappy and more maladjusted than those who remain in their original social class position.

HEALTH LIFE CHANCES

Health life chances like all other life chances are largely determined by social class attitudes and have been very fully documented by Susser and Watson (1962) following social research into medical treatment.

The middle class are more health conscious than the working class, and they are more prepared to accept medical advice than the working class and are more likely to act upon the advice. The working class are more prepared to act on the advice of their neighbours.

These social class differences towards health can affect the child's life chances even before he is born, as the Newsons' study (1965) shows, and as is further and more particularly illustrated by Rathbone (1973). Attendance at antenatal classes, she finds, is more common among middle-class mothers than working-class mothers who were in the majority of those women who refused to participate in the classes.

The better start-off for the new baby born into a middle-class family is indicated in the findings that 82 per cent of those mothers who attended the classes had 'A' (highest) rating babies and there were significant differences in the conditions of the babies at birth. A mother who has attended classes seems also to have a slightly better chance of managing her life with the baby in a happy and efficient way. The finding of poorer maternal care in the refusal group, Rathbone suggests, 'may be considered further confirmation of the tendency for the children in the lower social classes to suffer more from common ills than children in the higher social classes. Such things as more need for hospital care', she concludes, 'would be expected to follow from the basically less vigilant outlook of these mothers'.

In a dental study conducted in Manchester, Dickson (1968) found that the middle class are much more concerned with preserving their teeth than the working class. 72 per cent of the middle class paid regular 6-monthly or yearly visits to the dentist, whereas only 26 per cent of the working class went once a year and 60 per cent only went when they had toothache.

Dickson deplores the fact that the middle class are making greater use of the dental service than the working class even though it is supposed to be a 'public' service. The importance of dental health does not seem to be accepted as much by the working class as the middle class either for themselves or their children.

They have more negative attitudes concerning children's dental treatment in the working class, particularly with regard to having baby teeth filled, as the typical view expressed was that 'they will come out anyway', a view which takes no account of 'the effect on the child's general health of decaying teeth, nor of the effect on his digestion of his inability to chew food properly, nor of the effect upon his permanent teeth of losing his first teeth early'. Indeed, Dickson argues, if it were not for the school dental service, working-class children would receive very little dental treatment at all.

I should point out that a very large proportion of the British population suffer a common physical handicap: Thirty-seven per cent of all adults over the age of 16 have lost all their teeth. There is a clear relationship between social class and total tooth loss, which increases progressively from 15 per cent in social class I to 47 per cent in social class V (Reid, 1977). About 743 000 working days were lost in 1975 as a result of dental and gum disease.

MENTAL AND PHYSICAL DISORDERS

Certain mental and physical disorders have also been found to be associated with social classes. Ruesch *et al.* (1946) found that 'delayed recovery and psychosomatic diseases are conditions affecting middle-class people and climbers, as contrasted with the conduct disorders affecting primarily the lower class and decliners'.

In a later study (1948), they found that social mobility was found to be an important factor in the aetiology of duodenal ulcers.

A review of the state of malnutrition in British society in the 1960s (Office of Health Economics, 1967) concludes that there is no doubt that evidence of optimum growth and fitness does demonstrate that health is related to social factors and that health and physique are directly related to social class. A fact which gives rise to concern when there is a good deal of evidence, the report says, to show that as health and physique deteriorate the percentage of still births and neonatal death rate increases. A good deal of evidence is also found to show that in large families the height of children is less than that for the average, or only child. There is, however, some recent evidence cited by the chief medical officer of the Department of

Health and Social Security (1974) following the analysis of an investigation among pre-school children in 1968 that the average dietary intake and heights and weights of children in larger families and those in social classes IV and V and in the lower income ranges are not different from those of children from small families in social classes I and II and where the income of the head of the household is higher.

Other nutritional studies on adults suggest social class links. Montegriffo (1971), following a survey on the incidence of obesity in the United Kingdom, shows that there is a higher incidence of obesity at an earlier age in male administrative, scientific and clerical workers than in male skilled or unskilled workers. There is no significant difference, however, in similar groups of women. Although this survey did not include the relatively poorer members of the social strata, Montegriffo concedes that 'here, the problems seem even more real'.

About 5 million people in England consult their general practitioner every year about a mental health problem and 600 000 receive specialist psychiatric services. Mental health problems account for 24 million lost working days per year (HMSO, 1976). The severity of the problem is further highlighted by the fact that 46.6 million prescriptions for tranquillisers, antidepressants and hypnotics were signed by general practitioners in England in 1973. In the same year, consumers in the United Kingdom were spending about as much on self-medication as the British National Health Service was paying to its medical staff.

It has recently been reported (Kendell, 1979) that mortality from cirrhosis of the liver is steadily rising and that the number of convictions for public drunkenness in England and Wales rose by 28 per cent (91 per cent in Scotland) from 1969 to 1975. In 1976, 5097 children under 18 were convicted for drunkenness.

Reid (1977) cites evidence showing that 46 per cent of the British population are frequent visitors to pubs and 49 per cent are frequent drinkers at home. A particular point of interest is that in social class I, 77 per cent are frequent drinkers at home.

Kendell has identified certain high risk groups with regard to alcoholism. The professional classes are in greatest danger. Publicans head the list with a mortality rate from cirrhosis of the liver 16 times the national average. Ship's officers, insurance brokers, restaurateurs, journalists and medical practitioners have a mortality from cirrhosis of the liver at least three times the national average.

WOMEN'S LOT IN SOCIETY

The pull in the two directions of 'career' and 'family' goes on practically throughout life for women and is discussed eruditely by Myrdal and Klein (1968). Even though they concede that women no longer have to direct their struggle for the right to work against external obstacles they hold that today 'the conflict has become "internalised" and continues as a psychological problem which may assume different variations and shades'.

The report *Justice or Prejudice!* (1968) documents discrimination against women in the law, particularly with regard to laws related to domicile, taxation and loss of services for children. The report expresses concern that a lower percentage of girls than boys take GCE 'A' levels and an even lower percentage of girls than boys pass the examinations which 'suggests that for many 'O' level GCE passes may be regarded as the pinnacle of achievement, despite any evidence of any lack of ability among girls'.

Due to quota systems 2989 boys and only 733 girls were admitted to medical schools in 1966. Oxford University admitted 2040 men and only 462 women: the respective numbers for Cambridge University were 2358 and 269.

'A much higher standard of scholarship', the report adds, 'is usually demanded of women students than men in order to secure admission'.

Fewer girls than boys have an opportunity to study scientific subjects at school 'not because of lack of ability but because they do not receive encouragement'. When the young woman scientist enters industry she usually finds she has to be better qualified than the men with whom she has to compete and 'the starting salary is likely to be about 10 to 15 per cent less than that for a man', the report adds.

In 1966, 36 per cent of all employees in Britain were women yet they represented only 11.7 per cent of the professions and 16 per cent of the managers but accounted for 37 per cent of the manual work force. The report found 'that much prejudice still exists against the working wife and the idea persists that marriage and motherhood virtually end a woman's career'.

Another report, *Discrimination Against Women* (1968), after citing similar evidence notes social class differences, and concludes that: 'In the professional and higher echelons of management in industry, there are still many barriers to be broken down . . . But it is significant that the agonies of choice between "mother and career woman", the problems of "role conflict" are posed mainly for the professional women. For the working-class woman such psychological complexities are a luxury; she works usually because she has to, and is rewarded in most cases with less than half of a man's average wage'.

Another report commissioned by the Association of Teachers in Technical Institutes (1970) shows clearly the manifest inequalities in education, training and employment of women and girls.

In every type of further education course, women were found to be in a minority whether full time, 'sandwich', or day release courses.

Although the report concedes that opportunities in education and employment for boys and girls are equal in the limited sense that very few education courses and jobs are barred to girls, it contends that the opportunities 'are not equal in respect of being equally used—and if opportunities are not being used, they might as well not be there for all the good they are doing'.

The clear awareness of the conflict of roles of mother and worker is explicit in Gavron's work (1968) in which she documents the conflicts of a group of housebound mothers.

However, although the conflict was shared equally by both working-class and middle-class mothers, other clear social class differences are noted. Over 90 per cent of the middle-class mothers had been educated or trained for some clearly defined occupation by the time they had become mothers and 77 per cent of those mothers intended to return to some kind of work. Only 19 per cent of the working-class mothers had had any kind of further training but 29 per cent had acquired some skills while working. Eighty-seven per cent intended to return to work and Gavron contends that many would inevitably work in unskilled jobs below their capacity and that, for the working-class mothers, 'the roles of wife and mother had clearly affected their attitude to training and work before marriage, a situation many now regretted'.

The middle-class mothers who were working (37 per cent) had managed to arrange part-time work to fit in with the needs of their children and the main reason for working among middle-class mothers was a 'combination of emotional and intellectual needs'. But the working-class mothers (29 per cent) were less successful at combining home and work activities and their main reason for working was a 'combination of financial, emotional and intellectual needs'. A survey of nursery school participation conducted in

Cambridge (1965) indicates that there 'was a slightly higher proportion from the "professional-managerial" classes using nursery schools than would be expected from the sample as a whole', which suggests that middle-class mothers can also make better use of this resource than the working-class wife. However, the gains for the child attending nursery school may not be so real. A report prepared by Tizard (1975) considered the proliferation of nursery schools in the 1970s to be a 'gigantic social hoax', as, contrary to expectations, nursery school education has no long-term effect on children's development. She argues that the programme of expansion of nursery schools 'engenders false hopes of equalising later on' which she holds is 'doomed to failure'.

'Nursery schooling, or particular forms of it, may', she concedes, 'help to develop the child's social and cognitive skills as well as add to the happiness of child and mother'. But the report adds that nursery schooling would be more effective if carried out in neighbours' houses because a class in a formal classroom setting is too large a unit for a small child to cope with easily.

Other social class differences were noted by Gavron. The life of the young middle-class mother is one that entails a fair amount of activity in which family and friends play an important part. She tends to extend her interests outside her nuclear family. For the working-class wife, the nuclear family was an 'inward-looking unit' from which contact with the outside world was considerably less than for the middle-class mother.

There is one life chance, however, of which women can almost claim exclusively over men—that is the chance of long life espectancy. 'The expectation of life at 65 (and also at 75) among men', Titmuss (1968) points out, 'has hardly changed at all'. The gains for women, however, are 'real' and at the age of 75, life expectancy for women rose by 15 per cent in the 1960s.

There is, however, a sting in the tale, for this increased life expectancy for women inevitably widens the differential between the sexes, especially after the age of 75 and this fact has important implications. It means 'more widows and longer periods of widowhood' and in due course this probably means that 'nearly 80 per cent of the increased population over 75 will be women, most of whom will have been widowed many years earlier'. It could be argued, however, that this longevity in women may well be a result of their own socialisation in that the tasks associated with a 'woman's role' such as sewing, cooking, housekeeping and the like provide her with an opportunity for physical and mental activity and personal fulfilment in her years of retirement that are not afforded to most men who commonly retire from active working life to a life of inactivity.

Whatever the reason, there is no doubt that in the years of retirement women appear to have a physically healthier existence than men, as Currie *et al.* (1974) indicate. In an urban general practice they found that men aged 70–72 suffered 3.4 'disease entities' compared to 3.1 for women. They summarise the woman's health life chances pertinently:

'By the age of 70 the ranks of men have been thinned out by killing diseases and women outnumber men by three to two. Myocardial infarctions have taken their toll and heart disease is now equally distributed in the sexes, but 25 per cent of the men have demonstrable peripheral vascular disease and another 25 per cent have chronic bronchitis as compared with 9 per cent and 7 per cent respectively for women . . ..'

However, even though women seem to have better health life chances than men, if a woman is or becomes physically handicapped she is more likely than a physically handicapped man to be placed in institutional care according to Miller and Gwynne (1972) who find that there is a greater demand for residential accommodation for women, due to a mix of socialisation and economic factors.

'Of the inmates who have been married, women outnumber men—partly because the caring role is socially defined as a feminine role and this makes it more appropriate for a wife to look after a disabled husband than vice versa. This is reinforced by financial aid. The disabled husband normally has some kind of pension which makes it at least possible, if difficult, for the wife to devote her time to looking after him . . . no corresonding financial help is available if it is the wife who is disabled'.

It was however anticipated that plans outlined in the government report *Equal Opportunities for Men and Women* (1973) once implemented by law would iron out some of the social inequalities suffered by women.

But, according to Davidson (1979), the Equal Opportunities Commission, in its evidence to the Royal Commission on the National Health Service, recorded: 'It has been suggested with considerable justification that there is a tendency for male doctors—that is the majority of doctors—to diagnose a patient from a male point of view. We therefore suggest a full review of the attitudes and treatment of women patients in the NHS and that an increase in the number of women in senior posts would constitute towards improvement'. In Davidson's view, the Commission might well have added a plea for an increase in women administrators as well, for, as he points out, in recent years women have become predominant among entrants to administrative training schemes in the NHS. The overwhelming majority of them are in clerical and secretarial grades. Only two women are area administrators in England and Wales, and out of some 3600 administrators above the level of principal administrative assistant in England only about 170 are women. 'What is less clear is why this extraordinary imbalance should have occured and what can be done about it. Is it as a result of discrimination pure and simple or are wider issues involved?' (Davidson, 1979).

Prejudice apart, Davidson is forced to conclude that one of the problems is that the NHS exists in a society that still expects women to subordinate their careers to their families when the reverse remains true of men: 'Sadly, underlying the argument is an extraordinary lack of hard information about the plight of women. There are no figures for how many women, compared with men, drop out of either the training scheme or the service once they are trained. Nor has anybody bothered to find out why women leave. To all intents and purposes it is a non-issue'.

Deviancy

Social groups create deviancy by making the rules whose infraction constitutes deviancy. This is the plausible contention of Becker (1963). Once the rules are infracted by an individual he is automatically labelled an outsider and offender as, Becker contends, 'deviance is not a quality of the act the person commits, but rather a consequence of the application by others of rules and sanctions to an "offender". The deviant is one to whom that label has successfully been applied: deviant behaviour is behaviour that people so label'.

In his analysis of the genesis of gradual addiction of the marihuana user, Becker shows that the addict has to learn the technique of getting 'high' and to learn to perceive the effects of the drug—that is he has to learn what being 'high' really is. The drug user becomes aware of certain symptoms after smoking and has to learn to enjoy these effects. This taste for pleasurable experience is, in Becker's view, socially acquired. The sensations must be defined as pleasurable, usually by other drug users, even though initially most marihuana users experience frightening and distasteful symptoms.

As use of the drug is forbidden by law, the user is forced to seek out supplies. This leads to secrecy in deviant groups and abandonment of conventional morality, as 'a person will feel free to use marihuana to the degree that he comes to regard conventional conceptions of it as the uninformed views of outsiders and replaces those conceptions with the "inside" view he has acquired through his experience with the drug in the company of others'.

Studies of prostitution cited by Heidensohn (1968) indicate that rudimentary 'apprenticeship systems' exist in prostitution as a recognised means for girls to learn the ways of prostitution which include the 'passing on of skills, tricks and techniques': behaviour that is considered 'normal' by the prostitute groups themselves. On the whole, however, 'women appear to be remarkably conformist, they seem to have consistently lower rates of deviance than men'.

The genesis of sexual deviancy may be associated with poor quality of maternal care in infancy, if the findings from the observations on monkeys made by the Harlows (1965) can be generalised to humans. Whilst accepting the authors' comments that 'men are not monkeys and monkeys will never be men' their evidence of the effects of social deprivation during infancy on subsequent sexual function and orientation may be relevant to the study of sexual deviancies in humans. Perhaps it may help towards accepting deviancy as part of the social organisation that has evolved in society, as Schofield (1965) puts it in his sociological study of homosexuality: 'It is part of the social cost'; and to get rid of deviancy it may be necessary to change the social structure. But as he points out many parts of the social structure are good and as society does not want to lose those, the only alternative perhaps is to accept deviancy as an inevitable fact of social life.

Rickards (1979) also points out that an unattractive feature of the 'homosexual subculture' is a tendency to adopt a ghetto existence and 'sometimes to sound too much persecuted'. This, he suggests, is the result of society's victimisation of homosexuals by making it difficult or impossible for them to hold positions of responsibility or authority. But he predicts that there will 'come a kinder day—if civilisation is allowed to survive and thrive—when homosexuality will attract no more attention than left-handedness'.

But deviancy, like all other social facts, defies generalisation, as Hargreaves (1967) suggests. His study of secondary school boys indicates that the school organisation of placing the boys into four streams fostered deviant and non-deviant behaviour. Peer group influence was very powerful. The higher the stream, the greater the tendency for high status to be associated with the attitudes, values and behaviour expected by the school, whilst in the lower streams, low status was negatively associated with conformity to the school's (society's) expectations. The low group (group D) members tended to align with each other against the school and its rules and there was a great deal of delinquency in this group: in fact they created a 'delinquent subculture' of their own. But in spite of his generalisations and conclusions Hargreaves admits that the 'major unsolved problem is to explain the existence of deviants in each subculture', as some boys in each of the peer groups deviated from their group's norms. Values internalised in the home, he postulates, might provide a reservoir of resistance against informal norms. 'Although the extremes can be clearly distinguished', he concludes 'there remains a large proportion of boys who, whilst tending towards one of the poles, cannot easily be contained in either'.

The participants in violent gangs are, in Yablonsky's view (1967), 'sociopathic'. He argues that the kind of gang to which a youth is drawn depends on his style of upbringing and that these basic societal roots of the problem of violence should not be minimised, as 'the violent-gang problem arises in a social system that has a multitude of complex socio-cultural dislocations'. But the power of the mass media in fostering deviance should not be underestimated and Hudson (1967) holds that emotive newspaper reporting was to some extent responsible for the extension of the 'Hell's Angels' phenomenon in North America by causing undue panic in certain towns. 'It gave the "outlaws" a symbol and rallying point. The one per cent would get together. They would form their own club and would probably wear the "1 per cent" as an insignia. In short, they would found the Hell's Angels'.

Deviant behaviour, Cohen (1966) so rightly asserts, is not an invention of sociologists: it is a fact of social life, as 'people in society define certain kinds of acts as violations of rules and certain individuals as rule breakers'; but the borderlines between deviance and conformity are somewhat obscure, as 'people themselves are sometimes unsure of themselves and sometimes cannot agree on what is deviant'. A view supported by West (1967) who concedes that reliable information about the phenomena of delinquency are hard to come by and as nobody expects any one explanation or treatment method to solve all health problems, no one should expect 'a single cure-all for delinquency'.

The view that society itself applies the label of deviant to certain acts was also noted by Durkheim (1964) in his study of the division of labour in which he asserts 'we must not say that an action shocks the common conscience because it is criminal, but rather that it is criminal because it shocks the common conscience'. The stigmatising effects of this labelling process on the identity and the social life of the individual has been well documented by Goffman (1968) in his study of stigma.

This view finds some support from Rickards (1979) who indicates that in modern research there is no incontrovertible proof that homosexuality is due to profound biochemical or genetic determinants, but that 'the causes of sexual inclination are multifactorial'. Homosexuality, he adds, spans all sections of society. 'This means that at least 1 in 20, and possibly as many as 1 in 10, of all men and women in the unscreened professions . . . as well as dockers and miners are predominantly homosexual'.

CULTURAL INFLUENCES

In the decade prior to 1976, close to half a million immigrants came to the United Kingdom from the New Commonwealth, including Pakistan.

Some of the problems associated with immigrant groups have recently been discussed by O'Brien (1979). 'With around one million Moslem immigrants, mostly from Pakistan, India and Bangladesh,' he says, 'Britain has one of the biggest Moslem communities outside the Islamic world'. He goes on to point out that whilst Islam is advancing in Iran and Pakistan, the moslem faith is fighting to keep its hold on Asian immigrants in Britain against the pressures of Western social and moral influences.

Central to this issue is the Moslem teaching which places Asian women in a state of purdah, living 'in Western eyes like prisoners in their own homes'. As a result of exposure to Western culture these young Asian women in Britain are now beginning to challenge the traditional Moslem teaching about the place of women, and to ask why they cannot be free to go out with boyfriends and spend evenings in clubs and discotheques.

As purdah begins with puberty, while the girls are still at school, the comprehensive system of education—which is mostly coeducational—presents a major challenge to Islamic teaching, O'Brien says, and adds: 'Islamic leaders are stepping up the fight for their faith'. They are setting up two single-sex secondary schools and local Islamic centres. But there remain 'widespread tensions in Asian communities and concern among spiritual leaders, because Moslem teaching on the position of women is fundamental to family and social life'.

The implications of socialisation for the individual are summarised in the diagrammatic model in Figure 3.1.

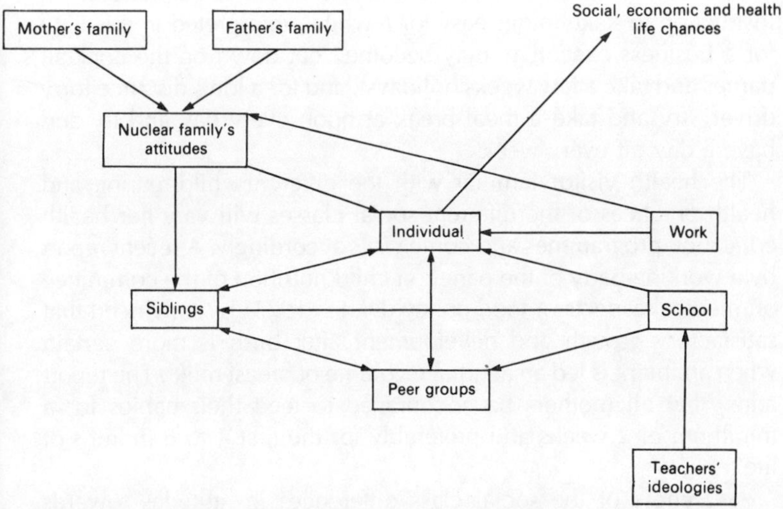

Figure 3.1 Factors affecting the individual's life chances.

Application to nursing

What use is all this information to the nurse? Some typical uses are discussed below.

When admitting a sick infant to hospital the paediatric nurse, knowing of the wide variation in traditions of feeding, weaning and toilet training in the different social classes, will ensure that information about these is obtained when the infant is admitted. This will prevent her from forcing the sick infant into an unfamiliar regime which will upset him and thereby impair his speedy recovery. As much as possible will be done to ensure that the infant has adequate love and affection during his hospitalisation, preferably from his parents, so as to avoid even temporary consequences of short-term deprivation.

The hospital nurse will foster tolerance to the apparently 'lazy' middle-aged working-class women who is reluctant to be mobilised after a hysterectomy, being aware that this could be due to the fact that it may be the first time since adolescenece that she has had an opportunity for a break from her home and work for 'a rest'. The hospital nurse will also pay particular care when she is interpreting medical and nursing instructions for the patient, bearing in mind the differences in life styles and life chances of the social classes. An instruction to 'take things easy for a while', interpreted in this light for a business executive, may become, 'cut down on the cocktail parties and take a few weeks holidays', and for a long-distance lorry driver, 'try and take a meal break at noon every day and try and have a day off every week'.

The health visitor familiar with the different child-rearing and health practices of the different social classes will vary her health education programmes and home visits accordingly. A recent report by a working party of the panel on child nutrition of the committee on medical aspects of food policy (DHSS, 1975) is 'convinced that satisfactory growth and development after birth is more certain when an infant is fed an adequate volume of breast milk'. The report adds 'that all mothers be encouraged to feed their babies for a minimum of 2 weeks and preferably for the first 4 to 6 months of life'.

Awareness of the social class differences in attitudes towards nudity will encourage the health visitor and the midwife to be particularly sensitive to their patient's feelings during the post-natal examination of a working-class mother's breast. The home nurse will carry out the catheter care of a working-class man with similar sensitivity and will not be unduly shocked when a middle-class man blatantly drops his trousers for an injection without any sign of embarrassment.

The insights of psychiatric nurses into the conditions of their patients will be enriched and enable them to more fully comprehend the possible social genesis of mental illness and deviancy and to care with greater sensitivity for individuals so afflicted and seeking care. They will also give more effective support to relatives.

The occupational health nurse could not function at all without sociological information.

All nurses will take care with their verbal and non-verbal communications with patients and clients in the light of what is known about the usual communication practices of the different social classes.

Finally, it will be obvious that all individuals in society are not equal and that inequality in life chances is to a great extent socially determined. If it is accepted that all men in society have a right to equal life chances, especially in health matters, then there is little point in treating unequals equally as this will perpetuate inequalities. A simple mathematical model demonstrates this (Figure 3.2). Unequals must therefore be treated unequally so that

Models of 'Equality'

	1	2	3	4	= Unequals
'weak'	1	1	1	1	= Treated Equally
	2	3	4	5	= Unequals

	1	2	3	4	= Unequals
'strong'	3	2	1	0	= Treated Unequally
	4	4	4	4	= Equals

Figure 3.2 Models of 'equality'

eventually all citizens' life chances will be as near equal as is possible. In the interests of social equality, therefore, positive discrimination may be necessary. This means that nurses must always weigh up priorities in the light of each individual's needs. The working-class mother may need more health visiting time than the middle-class mother. The working-class child may need more dental health education than the middle-class child. The working-class man may need to have longer convalescence in an institution after surgery than a middle-class man. In the allocation of resources, midwifery services in highly working-class areas will need adequate units for intensive care of neonates. In areas with a great deal of social mobility there may be a particular need for community psychiatric care facilities. In areas with a high percentage of elderly in the population there will be need for appropriate geriatric and psychogeriatric services, and so on. These are facts and perspectives which nurses must take to the health care planning teams in which they participate, as befits members of the major caring profession.

Sociological information can also be used by the nurse in her role as a health educator. This educational role of the nurse should not be underestimated. Once nurses have a personal commitment to health education, they will recognise that this entails team work and that the other members of the team will not necessarily be health care workers. Other members of society contribute towards the development of values and ideals of individuals: the family, clan, race, peers and colleagues as well as 'significant others' such as immigrant group leaders, local union officials, managers, teachers and so on. This was pointed out by Waddington (1977) in his discussion of the relationship between social class and the use of health services in Britain.

An important aspect of the nurse's role as educator is giving information. Skeet (1969) has demonstrated the failure of nursing staff to communicate with patients or relatives, most of whom had been given totally inadequate information about the state of their health and the treatment they would require at home. Yet Baly (1975) makes the point quite forecefully that nearly all research into hidden poverty and undisclosed sickness shows that many people, particularly the old, are not aware of the services to which they are entitled and are often too frightened or too proud to ask. This is particularly true among members of the lower social classes.

Oswin (1978) has also made a plea to health care professionals to give better information about welfare services to the physically handicapped of whom about one million, living in England and Wales, are slipping through the 'holes in the welfare net'.

Knowledge, although useful, is not enough in itself for the nurse to function adequately. It can only be applied when the nurse uses her practical and social skills. But like good nursing skills, sociological knowledge can prove a worthy means towards improving the quality of nursing and health care; skills and knowledge are complementary.

REFERENCES

Baly, M.E. (1975) *Professional Responsibility in Community Health Services.* Aylesbury: H M & M.

Becker, H.S. (1963) *Outsiders.* London: Collier-Macmillan.

Burt, C. (1975) *The Gifted Child.* London: Hodder & Stoughton.

Carter, M. (1966) *Into Work.* Pelican.

Cohen, A.H. (1966) *Deviance and Control.* Prentice Hall.

Cooley, C.H. (1909) *Social Organisation.* New York: Harper & Row.

Cox, C.B. & Dyson, A.E. (1969) *A Fight for Education.* London: The Critical Quarterly Society.

Currie, G. *et al.* (1974) Medical and social screening of patients aged 70–72 by an urban general practice health team. *British Medical Journal,* 13th April.

Davidson, N. (1979) Prejudice that faces women as managers. *Health and Social Services Journal,* **4631,** 322–324.

Dickson, S. (1968) Class attitudes to dental treatment. *British Journal of Sociology,* June.

Downes, D. & Fowler, F. (1965) *Educating for Uncertainty.* Fabian tract 364, October.

Douglas, J.W.B. (1964) *The Home and the School.* London: MacGibbon & Kee.

Durkheim, E. (1951) *Suicide* (revised edn.). Glencoe, Illinois: Free Press.

Durkheim, E. (1964) *The Division of Labour in Society* (revised edn.). London: Collier-Macmillan.

Engels, F. (1939) *The German Ideology.* New York: International Publishers.

Gavron, J. (1968) *The Captive Wife.* Pelican.

Goffman, E. *The Presentation of Self in Everyday Life.* Harmondsworth: Penguin.

Goffman, E. (1968) *Stigma.* Pelican.

Hargreaves, D.H. (1967) *Social Relations in a Secondary School.* London: Routledge.

Harlow, M.K. & H.F. (1965) An analysis of love. *The Listener,* 18th February.

Heidensohn, F. (1968) The deviance of women: a critique and an enquiry. *British Journal of Sociology,* June.

Her Majesty's Stationary Office (1977) *Prevention and Health: Everybody's Business.* London: HMSO.

Hunson, J. (1967) *Hell's Angels.* New English Library.

Jackson, B. & Marsden, D. (1966) *Education and the Working Class.* Harmonsworth: Pelican.

Kendell, R.E. (1979) Alcoholism: a medical or political problem? *British Medical Journal,* **6160,** 1, 367–371.

Lipset, S.M. & Bendix, R. (1959) *Social Mobility in Industrial Society.* University of California Press.

Moddock, J. (1967) Station in Life. *British Journal of Sociology,* December.

Marsden, D. (1974) How far on the road to educational equality? Child Poverty Action Group, London, Autumn.

Marx, K. & Engels, F. (1888) *Communist Party Manifesto.* Moscow: Progress Publishers.

Miller, E.J. & Gwynne, G.V. (1972) *A Life Apart.* London: Tavistock.

Montegriffo, V.M.E. (1971) A survey of the incidence of obesity in the U.K. *Postgraduate Medical Journal,* June, supplement.

Myrdal, A. & Klein, V. (1968) *Women's Two Roles: Home and Work*. London: Routledge.
Newson, J. & E. (1965) *Patterns of Infant Care in an Urban Community*. Harmondsworth: Pelican.
O'Brien, R.B. (1979) Moslem leaders fight to save faith in Britain. *Daily Telegraph*, 26th February.
Oswin, M. (1978) *Holes in the Welfare Net*. Plymouth: Macdonald & Evans.
Rathbone, B. (1973) Focus on new mothers. Royal College of Nursing.
Reid, I. (1977) *Social Class Differences in Britain: a Source Book*. London: Open Books.
Richards, F. S. (1979) Victims of Society. *Nursing Mirror*, **149,** (18), 28–30.
Ruesch, J. *et al.* (1946) *Chronic Disease and Psychological Invalidism: a Psychosomatic Study*. New York: Holber.
Ruesch, J. *et al.*, (1948) *Duodenal Ulcer*. University of California Press.
Schofield, M. (1965) *Sociological Aspects of Homosexuality*. London: Longman.
Sorokin, P.A. (1964) *Social and Cultural Mobility*. London: Collier-Macmillan.
Shaw, R. (1969) *Culture and equality—the role of Adult Education*. Keele University.
Skeet, M. (1969) *Home from Hospital*. London: Dan Mason.
Susser, M.W. & Watson, W. (1962) *Sociology in Medicine*. Oxford University Press.
Swift, D.F. (1967) Social class, mobility—ideology and 11+ success. *British Journal of Sociology*, June.
Titmuss, R.M. (1964) *Introduction to 'Equality'* (R.H. Tawney). London: Allen & Unwin.
Titmuss, R.M. (1968) *Commitment to Welfare*. London: Allen & Unwin.
Tizard, B. (1975) *Early Childhood Education*. National Foundation for Educational Research.
Tonnies, F. (1961) *Custom: an Essay on Social Codes*. Glencoe, Illinois: Free Press.
Waddington, I. (1977) The relationship between social class and use of health services in Britain. *Journal of Advanced Nursing*, **2,** 609–619.
Weber, M. (1947) *The Theory of Social and Economic Organisation*. New York.
West, D.J. (1967) *The Young Offender*. Harmondsworth: Pelican.
Yablonsky, L. (1967) *The Violent Gang*. Harmondsworth: Pelican.
Report of the Central Advisory Council for Education (The Crowther Report). HMSO, 1959.
A survey of Nursery School Participation in Cambridge. Cambridge Association for the Advancement of State Education 1965.
Children and Their Primary Schools HMSO, 1967.
Malnutrition in the 1960s? Office of Health Economics, 1967.
Discrimination Against Women. National Labour Women's Advisory Committee 1968.
Justice or Prejudice? National Federation of Business and Professional Women's Clubs of Great Britain and Northern Ireland 1968.
Education, Training and Employment of Women and Girls. Association of Teachers in Technical Institutes 1970.
Equal Opportunities for Men and Women. Department of Employment 1973.
On the State of the Public Health. Chief Medical Officer's Report, HMSO, 1974.
Present-day Practice in Infant Feeding. Report of a working party of the panel on child nutrition of the committee on medical aspects of food policy, Department of Health and Social Security, 1975.
Report on the Work of the Employment Medical Advisory Service. HMSO, 1975.

4

Socialisation in the hospital social system: becoming a nurse and patient

A hospital is a network of the expectations of a number of individuals: administrators, cleaners, doctors, nurses, patients, porters and so on. These expectations pull together to form a new social reality, making the hospital, more than a mix of buildings and people, a system of social action. The historical influences which have moulded the way the pattern of actions and expectations has been formed cause each hospital to take on a character of 'personality' of its own. People will consider it bureaucratic or warm, or if it has a long history as a teaching centre, as charismatic. This social system of the hospital is therefore built up over a time, and how the various individuals within the hospital perform is influenced by its social structure.

The concept of a social system describes one of the ways of patterning human behaviour. It therefore can contribute to a fairly accurate analysis and prediction of the behaviour of nurses and patients in hospital. For people interacting in a hospital setting appear to set up patterns of behaviour and expectations. As the interaction becomes less random, structure-positions are created that are invested with certain sets of behaviour expectations and sometimes with special rank, such as senior nurse or convalescent patient.

Among others, two groups of individuals (input) enter the hospital social system through which they are processed over time as nursing students and patients and eventually leave the system (output) as trained nurses and cured/convalescent/rehabilitated/terminally sick individuals respectively.

As nurses and patients share the same social system in the hospital it is appropriate to consider their socialisation in the same context.

Social status appear in clusters in social systems. The nursing officer for example is in a social status position in the hospital and a whole set of other positions result from this occurrence, which have a special pattern of relationships to each other. The social positions of patient, charge nurse, staff nurse, student nurse, unit administrator, domestic supervisor and medical registrar all appear with the nursing officer position and the actions of all the people in this cluster are specially relevant for the nursing officer. These people are her role partners and the way they perform will affect the nursing officer's performance. In fact, the same could be argued for each individual role holder. Trouble arises when the role partners have different ideas about the appropriate behaviour, and rights and responsibilities of the various social groups, but when the group shares common ideas a smooth, functional team emerges.

As patients interact with nurses more than with any other professional health care worker over each 24-hour period, it could be argued that compatibility in their ideas about their respective social status is of crucial importance to the smooth functioning of the health care team of which the patient is a significant member.

It is, of course, an oversimplification to consider each person as having only one social position, viz. that of nurse or patient, in society, as each can also act in the social positions of citizen, enemy, son, husband, mason and so on, a combination of social poisitions called *status-set*.

The concept 'status-set' indicates the difficulty inherent in being a patient or a student nurse if those role holders are supposed to be docile and subordinate when the same individuals may be a bank manager and grandmother respectively.

That social positions, once created, are very real and exert a strong influence on the individual is made clear by Mumford and Skipper (1967) who argue that 'structure positions and their patterning makes for somewhat orderly groups even among strangers, and orderly institutions and organisations rather than collectivities of persons engaged in random behaviour and bumping into each other like marbles tossed on a floor'.

The 'realness' of social status, however, can create some difficulties as the labelling of one individual as 'nurse' and another as 'patient' tends to create stereotype ideas as to what is or should be the appropriate behaviour for the role. This can be dysfunctional for patient care if, for example, the individual who is a nurse is perceived by the patient to be a charismatic angel of mercy and the individual who is a patient is perceived by the nurse to be an unquestioning, subordinate and dependent individual. For then both nurse and patient may endow the holder of the role of nurse with the right to say to the holder of the role of patient, in respect of treatment and care: 'Yours to do or die, but not to know the reason why!'

Sharing socialisation processes

Nurses and patients also share similar socialisation processes in the hospital. They both undergo a process of 'role-stripping' which divests them of the symbols associated with their previous social roles of, for example, adolescent girl and docker. This process is carried out during the ritual of exchanging the clothes associated with their former social roles for those of a uniform, in the case of the student nurse, and pyjamas and dressing gown, in the case of the patient. Both are also to some extent divested of their personal identities by a labelling process. The student nurse if given the (honorary) title of 'nurse' and the sick individual labelled 'patient' and often given an index number as well.

The concept of role-stripping and its implications is vividly illustrated by Goffman (1968) when he cites the Holy Rule of Saint Benedict to describe the admission of a novice to the Benedictine order:

'Then forthwith, there in the oratory, be he divested of his own garments with which he is clothed and be he clad in those of the monastry. Those garments of which he is divested shall be placed in the wardrobe, there to be kept, so that if, perchance, he should ever be persuaded by the devil to leave the monastry (which God forbid), he may be stripped of the monastic habit and cast forth'.

Social distance

Both nurse and patient inevitably experience 'social distance' in the social system and this is a further reason for studying the socialisation of the nurse and patient in the same context. Patients and nurses are individuals in different and distinct social groups which, even though they are geographically near in the hospital, are distinctly separate social entities; a social group of patients and a social group of nurses separated by social distance.

The concept of social distance and other associated concepts are elaborated by Sorokin (1964). In his view 'human beings who are members of the same social groups and who within each of these groups have the same functions, are in an identical social position. Men who differ in these respects from each other have different social positions. The greater the resemblance of the positions of the different men, the nearer they are toward each other in social space. The greater and more numerous are their differences in these respects, the greater is the social distance between them'.

Indeed, on this analysis it could be argued that social distance also exists between nursing students and trained nurses who also form two distinct social groups in hospital.

BECOMING A NURSE

According to the findings of MacGuire, reported to a London conference (Smith 1969), interest in nursing develops early in individuals who want to become nurses. A third of all 18-year-old girls, she says, are interested in nursing at some time in their lives. This interest is at its peak in the 15 to 18 year old, but needs to be fostered.

In the past, recruitment to nursing has, MacGuire indicates, been concentrated on the 'single grammar school girl', but, she argues, older women have a more positive attitude to nursing. And a considerable minority of men also have positive attitudes to nursing. In view of widespread trends among women, such as earlier marriage and motherhood, MacGuire contends that men in nursing may prove a 'better bet'. The positive attitudes of men to nursing have been further demonstrated by Brown and Stones (1973) who find that men in nursing do not fit into a 'technical rather than comfort role' and that they are 'more realistic than female entrants in appreciating the caring role of the nurse'.

Other countries are increasingly becoming aware of the value of this atptitude of some men for nursing. It is a source of great pride to Danish nurses that they have not lost any male nurse who started and completed training. Their first 80 are apparently doing very well (Smith 1969). And a pioneer basic nursing course offered in the City University of New York to fireman and policeman about to retire and start a second career has proved so popular that other colleges are now offering similar courses (Smith 1974). In fact, there was a hundred per cent pass-rate in the qualifying examinations of the pioneer course students.

A major factor bothering MacGuire is the great deal of documented confusion about the desired 'end product' of basic nursing courses.

The concept 'nurse'

The concept nurse is defined by Travelbee (1966) as a 'human being sharing in common the human conditions of all peoples . . . the nurse possesses a body of specialised knowledge and ability to use it for the purpose of assisting other human beings to prevent illness, regain health, or to maintain the highest maximal degree of health'.

Travelbee contends that the nurse, in the process of acquiring specialised knowledge and professional education, is an individual who has been profoundly and irrevocably changed. New skills are developed by her ability to learn and apply scientific knowledge; but the nursing student is also profoundly affected by being confronted with the illness, suffering and death of individuals in a way, Travelbee holds, 'that an adolescent or young adult entering another occupational field' is not.

As a result of the observations on the effects on individuals of illness and suffering and inferences made from these observations, the nurse eventually perceives illness to be 'real' and not 'comfortable abstractions'.

'Suffering also ceases to be a theoretical concept', Travelbee further argues 'when perceived as a crying, moaning, screaming human being, and dying becomes an undeniably shattering reality to the nurse caring for the moribund individual'.

The repeated exposure to illness, suffering and death affects the nurse and by being confronted with her patients' vulnerability, she is forced to come to terms with 'the compelling force of her own vulnerability'. Her ability to perceive, respond to and care for patients will, in Travelbee's view, be determined by the nurse's manner of dealing with her own crises of vulnerability and the way she learns to cope with her own feelings.

'Thus the crises of vulnerability can determine the nurse's capacity to realise her own humanity as well as her capacity to respond to, and care for' the patient, Travelbee argues.

She further argues that the term nurse is a 'label' which can have a dehumanisation effect if it leads to the perception of 'nurse' as a stereotype and not as someone who is a unique individual. The stereotype, Travelbee contends, is the greatest barrier to allowing the nurse to perceive and respond to the human being in the patient, as well as acting as a barrier to helping others to respond to the human being who is a nurse.

Nursing conscience

A significant change that occurs in the nurse during her professional socialisation, Travelbee postulates, is the development of a 'nursing conscience' resulting from absorption by the nursing student of certain belief and value systems. This 'nursing conscience' gives rise to a particular type of guilt in a nurse, because she is a nurse, 'when realising that she has not fulfilled her responsibilities'. This 'nursing conscience' is not, in her view, distinct from conscience *per se*, but represents one aspect of it.

The concept of 'nursing conscience' is, in my view, another way of conceptualising what is commonly known as the 'professional ethic' but it also has conceptual similarities to the concept of 'collective conscience' described by Durkheim (1964) in his discussion of mechanical solidarity society:

'The totality of beliefs and sentiments common to average citizens of the same society forms a determinate system which has its own life; one may call it the *collective* or *common conscience* . . . It is, in effect, independent of the particular conditions in which individuals are placed: they pass on and it remains . . . It is, thus, an entirely different thing from particular consciences, although it can be realised only through them.'

BASIC NURSING EDUCATIONAL INFLUENCES ON THE STUDENT

In a large-scale study of 19 student nurse intake groups in five schools of nursing in Oxford, MacGuire (1968) shows how, because their 'preliminary training school' was isolated from the rest of the organisation the new nursing students were left to 'draw on the resources of the group for their entertainment, intellectual stimulation and morale' which gave rise to the strong influence of the 'set' (intake group) throughout the training period. The 'set' shares common inititation procedures and consists of a group in which, of necessity, the individual student is highly involved. 'It *institutionalises* the type of relationship which grows up spontaneously in other situations among groups undergoing courses of training'.

In the preliminary training school, MacGuire shows how a strong sense of community develops and how strong bonds of friendship between groups and cliques of nursing students are built up. During this introductory period to nursing the close interaction of the 'set' produces shared patterns of behaviour, and shared attitudes towards study and practical work and towards nursing.

'By the end of the preliminary school the student nurses certainly feel that the set is an important unit to them. They share the concept of set-equivalence, by which I mean that any one member of a set is regarded as a substitute for any other . . . to such an extent that any criticism of a particular set member is taken as a criticism of the group.'

During the three-year training period some formal effort is made to ensure that the 'set' remains a viable unit. They have study-blocks together, for example. But, frequently the hospitals, having created the 'set', fail to provide for the continuing existence of the group as a physical entity which may, in MacGuire's view, be a factor causing nursing students to give up their training.

In the hospital, MacGuire finds, there is a hierarchy of sets and the principle on which the sets are stratified is that of 'occupational skill'. Mobility in the system is based on the principle of 'social age'—that is the length of time the individual nurse has been associated with the hospital.

The initial size of the 'set' appears to have some relationship with students withdrawing from training. Small intake groups are less likely to survive intact than large intake groups. Students recruited into intake groups of less than 10 are nearly twice as likely to withdraw as those students recruited into intake groups of 10 or more.

Nursing as a social system, MacGuire suggests, is analogous to the Samoan age-group structured society which Margeret Mead (1966) has described. In Samoa, society is stratified according to age and the socialisation process is not based on an interchange between adult and child but between the age group immediately above and the age group immediately below.

Although she does not acknowledge it, MacGuire's concept of 'set' is analogous to the concept of 'primary group', described by Cooley and associates (1939), in every respect except size. Primary groups are 'fundamental in forming the social nature and ideals of the individual. The result of intimate association, psychologically is a certain fusion of individualism in a common whole, so that one's very self, for many purposes at least, is the common life and purpose of the group' Perhaps the simplest way of describing this wholeness is by saying that it is a "we"; it involves the sort of sympathy and mutual identification for which "we" is the natural expression'.

MacGuire (1969) concedes elsewhere in a report on wastage of nursing students, which she prepared after a review of over sixty investigations on the withdrawal of nursing students from nursing courses that: 'Exactly what it is about hospitals which affects outcomes for students . . . is still open to enquiry . . . From the point of view of the explanation of attrition rates for various categories of learners what seems to be required is the development of indices for the measurement of hospitals as contexts for learning'.

The concept of nursing evolves

In a review of literature on nursing, Hanrahan (1970) holds that the 'concept of nursing' evolves in response to varying cultural determinants and that these will inevitably influence the pattern and type of training which a student nurse receives. She finds that Irish nursing students, on the whole, see their basic nursing courses not as ends in themselves but as prerequisites to advanced post-basic nursing courses, but adds that a fair number of nursing students, having internalised the norms of the ward situation, have 'incorporated them into their own ways of thinking and behaving, conforming therefore to the institutionalised goal of service rather than to the educational goal of training'. But, of course, it is not necessarily deplorable that nursing students should see education as a means towards an end rather than an end in itself. It might be argued that perhaps those nursing students who see it as a means towards an end have appraised the objectives of nursing education realistically.

A point that comes through very strongly in a study carried out by Lamond (1974) is that the first year of training is seen by virtually all nurses to be the most important year in the introduction of all aspects of nursing. The first year is seen as the 'most suitable for initiation' by the majority of registered nurses interviewed. She concludes that the new nursing student is therefore likely to be 'flooded with many new impressions and is introduced to a wealth of new expectations, for which she has to learn the rights and obligations before she becomes recognisable as a "nurse"'. More competence in the learning process is expected in the first year of training, Lamond holds, than in any of the other years of a three year basic nursing course.

In an effort to overcome some of the difficulties inherent in basic nursing education courses, Birch (1975) argues that it is necessary 'to relate to each learner personally, and to gear the programme of learning to give maximum opportunity for discussing individual problems. Attempts to build up a diagnostic picture for each learner, it is hoped, will provide a basis, however rudimentary, for further exploration and research'. His assertion may be correct, but one of the main problems bedevilling the nursing profession is that very little is known about the kinds of people who do *not* leave nursing courses and who subsequently follow a nursing career successfully. There is, however, a good deal of impressionistic evidence that the profession has a niche for many types and the Briggs Report (*Report of the Committee on Nursing* 1972) gives some support to this view in its conclusion that 'no obstacles should be placed in the way of suitable applicants with a spectrum of initial academic qualification from average intelligence to the highest'.

However, there are some gaps in the professional socialisation of nurses, as Norton (1972) indicates in her research on the design of equipment used by nurses. She finds that most nurses have little understanding of their responsibilities in this area.

Particular problems in advanced basic courses

There is some evidence to suggest that nursing students undergoing advanced basic and undergraduate nursing courses have greater professional socialisation problems than other nursing students taking traditional kinds of basic courses.

In her evaluation of the first advanced basic nursing course to be offered in the United Kingdom, by the Hammersmith Hospital School of Nursing and Battersea College of Advanced Technology (now University of Surrey), Bryden (1969) notes the concerns of the early student pioneers. 'Many students, particularly from the first two groups, initially had difficulty in appreciating fully the aims of the course. This was because of the number of people they met, both inside and outside the hospital, who were resistant to change and could not see any advantage in the new pattern of training'.

Sister Mary Hubert (1967), in a study of four British basic university nursing courses, notes that the students taking these courses 'were frequently subjected to embarrassment, to subtle forms of rejection. They were rejected for being less skilful, for exercising independent judgement, or for seeing the patient primarily as an individual'.

These sentiments are further endorsed by a former undergraduate nursing student of the University of Edinburgh who, speaking at a conference in 1973, claimed that she had experienced conflict as a student due to her enthusiasm about being a pioneer on the one hand and yet sensing a lot of undercurrents at the hospital on the other hand (Smith 1973). This, she holds, was because 'colleagues and superiors tended to be baffled about the need for high-level education'. A subsequent speaker, a ward sister, agreed that the majority of nursing undergraduates were first-rate and that they learned quickly and retained what they had learned. But, she conceded, the nursing undergraduate was a challenge to ward sisters as they 'felt a little insecure because of their own perceived lower intelligence and poorer powers of expression'.

However, I do not think that this state of affairs is typical of nursing in the United Kingdom alone as, during my own observations of nursing in North America (Smith 1974), with over sixty years experience in undergraduate nursing courses, I still detected some ambivalence among members of the nursing profession. The following quotations illustrate the prevailing ambivalence.

'The reason why so many baccalaureate nurses don't come to hospitals is because they can't cope with hard work' (Director of Nursing).

'There was much in the diploma programmes that was good. We lost a lot . . . don't throw the baby out with the bath water' (Assistant Professor of Nursing).

'I think many of the nursing professors are teaching in universities because they don't like nursing' (Hospital School of Nursing Teacher).

'The baccalaureate students are certainly very knowledgeable, but I would be happier if they were exposed to the clinical situation for longer periods' (Assistant Director of Nursing).

'Of course, the baccalaureate nurses are better than hospital diploma graduates' (Professor of Nursing).

'To be honest, we have to advise our brightest candidates to apply for a college course' (Director of a Hospital School of Nursing):

INFLUENCES AFTER QUALIFYING AS A NURSE

As McLemore and Hill (1966) say, the process of professional socialisation does not finish when basic nursing education programmes are completed. 'Conflicts in definitions of the nursing role may be brought even more sharply into focus as the neyphyte commences her professional career and moves through various stages in it, generating a continuous potential for attitudes formation and change'.

On this assumption they generate four basic hypotheses about the post-basic professional socialisation of nurses. They postulate that nurses holding a degree can be characterised by a greater acceptance of human-relations attitudes than non-graduate nurses: that recently-trained nurses are characteristically more likely to accept human-relations attitudes than nurses who trained some time ago: that the greatest impact of the influence of human-relations philosophy has been made on nurse-managers in large hospitals; and that 'the forces which differentially affect supervisory nurses in large hospitals also impinge unequally upon those of high and low authority, independent of hospital size'. In other words, that the nurse in a high authority position is more likely to be concerned with organisational and managerial problems than a nurse supervising the nursing services on a clinical unit.

These four hypotheses were supported to a great extent by research findings from which two nurse-manager 'types' were derived. *Type X*—those nurses in positions of high authority who are recently qualified graduates and who are employed in large hospitals. *Type Y*—those nurses in lower positions of authority who qualified earlier and are non-graduates and who are employed in small hospitals. The findings also show that there is a differential exhibition of the attitudes which are related to the elements of human-relations philosophy in the two types of nurse-manager. Type X demonstrate greater degrees of 'democracy', 'functional orientation' and 'willingness to initiate action' than Type Y nurses.

McLemore and Hill readily concede that arguments could be made that these results may be produced by both selection and the socialisation process, as it is plausible that those who 'tend to display the attitudes of Type X nurses are more likely to be selected for specific roles in nursing'. Nevertheless they hold that the weight of their evidence suggests 'that socialisation is substantially the more powerful process'.

The importance of continued professional development through education is demonstrated by the Briggs Report which stresses that: 'Education should be regarded as a continuous process under unified control'.

I suspect that the proliferation of approval of one-year nurse-tutor courses in colleges of education in the 1970s by the General Nursing Councils in Great Britain is also based on an implicit recognition of the importance of education in professional socialisation. Prior to the introduction of one-year courses only two-year nurse-tutor courses were available which included courses in biological, medical and (very little) social sciences. But these courses in my view, did not emphasise the central position of the art and science of *nursing*. As a result, many, like me, probably found the course dysfunctional in that as newly qualified nurse-tutors there was an undoubted tendency to consider one's students moronic if they could not grasp the concepts of carbon dioxide carriage, osmosis and growth of micro-organisms, taught in isolation from and not in the context of the nursing process.

In the one-year tutor's course the emphasis in the curriculum is on education of nurses and the *teaching of nursing* and that is how it should be. A survey conducted among teachers of nursing by the General Nursing Council for England and Wales (1975) indicates that only 46 per cent of the respondents felt that the teaching courses for nurses had adequately prepared them for the task of teaching nursing. The biggest deficit was in planning and interpreting research of which 87 per cent of the respondents said they were less than adequately prepared. In those circumstances, how can nursing ever become a research-based profession?

Return to reality

If there has been a drift away from realistic objectives in nursing education there are signs that, at least in North America, nursing education is 'showing signs of becoming more clinically oriented as . . . noted in the dissertation topics prepared for the ever growing graduate courses at master and doctorate level' (Smith 1974). This is particularly noteworthy in the 'role' courses in the new master's degree course offered in the Boston University School of Nursing. This intensive focus on 'role' is offered, Hull (1971) declares, because clarity of understanding and high quality of performance in particular nursing roles are characteristic of the skilled nurse-practitioner.

' "Role" denotes many socially imposed modes of behaviour that a person accepts and internalises during his lifetime. Professional roles change with time and growth,' she holds. Professional socialisation in nursing is thus an ongoing process throughout the professional life of the nurse.

Hopefully, some of this ethos will 'rub off' from the master-in-nursing courses innovated in the University of Manchester in the early 1970s and from the master's degree in nursing education innovated in the University of Edinburgh in 1975.

The innovator: a 'deviant' case

If the goal of nursing education is perceived to be that of producting nurses who will be innovators, Ruano (1971) argues, this means that nursing educators have taken on the task of producing deviants—'one whose behaviour is different from the norm as defined by the setting'.

The goal given to nursing educators, she says, is to produce nurses who, whilst accepting the traditional goals of nursing, are innovative enough to find new and more effective means of achieving these goals, given that nursing functions in an ever changing health care system.

But the educator is blocked because the trained nurse in charge of the ward where the student goes for clinical experience does not grant permission to disrupt or change ongoing patient care.

This results in the educator structuring the student's learning experience so that she can become an innovator in the student setting and not in the real world of health care. The newly qualified nurse, as a result, Ruano contends, is only able to be innovative in 'atypical patient situations' and she is certainly not 'socialised to function as an innovator in a setting in which creativity and change are more frequently punished than rewarded' as is generally the case, she argues, in health care settings.

Because change is more likely to be 'punished' the newly qualified nurse finds it impossible to function as a 'deviant' innovator, Ruano argues, and within a short time appears to take on the belief and attitude systems of her nursing colleagues.

Those who continue to function as 'deviants' take up nursing positions such as public health nursing, unit nursing officers, clinical teachers and research posts 'in which conflict with existing practices is minimised'. But unfortunately there are not enough of these posts to go round and in any case, Ruano points out, the potential innovators who take these posts limit their potential for change by reducing the visibility of their behaviour. She holds that changes both in the socialisation process of nurses and in the health care system are necessary before nurses can be expected to act as innovators. It is not enough, she argues, to change the system so that deviancy will be rewarded but to change the fact that 'nurses have been socialised to avoid the risk of failure'.

Negative sanctions are rightly imposed on the nurse who gives unsafe nursing care. But negative sanctions are also imposed on the nursing student who elects to spend the major part of her time talking to an apprehensive patient rather than 'getting the work done'. Negative sanctions are also imposed on the nursing student who does not complete her nursing care study assignment on time, because of attempting to meet the social needs of a debilitated elderly woman, and so on.

This lack of attention to the many dimensions of failure, Ruano holds, 'produces an atmosphere in which failure to achieve any kind of goal is viewed synonymously with poor practice and is not tolerated'. This is the kind of atmosphere which encourages most nurses to avoid taking any risks. Those who are more courageous, like the persistent innovators, seek out the relatively isolated patient care situations where their 'failures' will not be seen but where their successes also will not be rewarded.

Innovators in nursing, on this analysis, will therefore not be produced and 'the socialisation process must be modified to focus on the many dimensions of failure'.

The nursing profession must, in Ruano's view, establish boundaries within which nurses can be expected to be innovators and must be rewarded for acting as such. But the profession is under no obligation to support the innovator unless that nurse maintains a primary concern with the forward movement of nursing, she adds.

An attempt must be made to minimise the isolation of innovators by providing them with knowledge about other nursing innovators. This will also make them more visible to other nursing colleagues who are less courageous and provide them with role-models. The profession should also, Ruano concludes, both use and spread the knowledge that is generated by these nurse innovators.

'Nursing has little choice regarding the assumption of responsibility for changing the changes that are occurring within the profession and the health care system. Indeed, the nurse must innovate change. However, alterations are needed in the health care system and the socialisation process of nurses if the attempts at innovation are to have an impact on the nursing profession and patient care.'

The lot of the innovator in nursing cannot be better illustrated than by quoting from the obituary of Mrs Ethel Bedford Fenwick, the instigator of registration for nurses and founder of the International Council of Nurses, cited by Bowman (1967):

'Strange it was that so great a reformer, the bestower of so many good things upon nurses, should receive so little gratitude from them. Her tremendous efforts on their behalf received scant appreciation from her colleagues, yet she zealously continued along her chosen path, often maligned, always eventually justified in her actions and decisions . . . like a true prophet she has little honour in her own country but the wise Americans know, love, and honour her and so do the nurses of many other lands . . ..'

BECOMING A PATIENT

One of the tasks of the nurse is to perceive and to respond to the human being who is a patient and therefore, as Travelbee (1966) points out, the concept 'patient' is a pivotal one in nursing. The term 'patient' is actually a label and a category and it may, like the label 'nurse', also denote a stereotype if the abstracted meanings of the concept of 'patient' are applied indiscriminately.

If the concept 'patient' becomes a broad generalisation covering *all* patients, Travelbee argues, the nurse may totally disregard the uniqueness of each individual human being who is a patient. John

Brown who is suffering from pneumonia is not Peter White who is suffering from haematuria who is not Michael Jones who is suffering from depression, and so on.

The meaning attached to the concept 'patient' and the nurse's perception of individual patients seem to have 'a reciprocal oscillating type of relationship', Travelbee argues. And the nurse's perception of the patient is a crucial factor in determining the quality and quantity of care he will receive, she holds.

Two very interesting reports prepared by Moores (1975) following observations in hospitals for the mentally handicapped support that view. He finds that individual nurses not only vary in their expectations of patients, which affects patient accomplishment, but also that some hospitals appear to possess more than their fair share of nurses who are 'optimists' while other hospitals in his study contain a disproportionate representation of nurses who are 'pessimists'. In the environment of the latter kinds of hospital, he finds, 'the patients are consequently unlikely to develop the necessary skills for a reasonable level of social activity.'

Moores also finds that a relatively small proportion of mentally handicapped patients receive a disproportionately large number of staff-patient interactions and holds that other groups of patients would merit similar levels of care and attention but do not receive it even though they need it most.

There is some evidence, Moores finds, 'that those who receive most staff-initiated interactions tend to be those who initiate most themselves'.

A nurse acts as she believes and thinks, and what she thinks and believes about her patients will be reflected in the care they receive. The actual labelling of a human being as a 'patient' may, Travelbee argues, be a dehumanising process as the concept 'patient' is 'an abstraction, a set of expectations personified by tasks to be performed, treatments to carry out, an illness, or a room number'. It therefore matters a great deal whether or not a nurse perceives an individual to be a 'unique human being' or a 'patient'. And Travelbee further argues that: 'The role of "nurse" needs to be transcended in order to perceive and relate as human being to human being, instead of "nurse" to "patient" . . . It is only in human to human relatedness, which means transcending roles, that a relationship is established . . ..'

The individual's response to being treated as a dehumanised 'patient' is affected by the individual's perception of threat and the techniques he normally uses to cope with threat—the most common emotional response being anger. This anger may be displaced onto another person, such as the nurse, with whom the patient feels safe. If not directed outwards the patient may become irritable, tense and restless, sad, apathetic or depressed. Occasionally he may develop 'transient somatic symptoms'.

But, as well as the factors already mentioned, the individual's response to the dehumanisation process will also be affected by his 'social class, position and financial status'. If his social and financial status is above average he will be better equipped to deal with the problem if it occurs, and if his complaints are not effective he can usually seek assistance elsewhere. But individuals in the lowest socio-economic group, Travelbee points out, 'are not well equipped with resources to deal with dehumanisation'. Many of the lowest socio-economic group, especially if aspects of health care have to be paid for, 'accept dehumanisation, many times without even publicly protesting'.

I can also confirm from my own experience that, on the whole, the majority of complaints about health care are made by the articulate and tenacious members of the middle class in the community, due, to some great extent, I am sure, to the fact that complaints are not treated seriously by the bureaucracy of health care organisation unless they are made in writing. However, the Davis Committee Report on Hospital Complaints procedure (1974) recommend many changes.

Nurses and others in hospitals should not retreat into self-righteous complacency if most surveys of patients' attitudes to their care generally indicate high levels of satisfaction. This may well be due to the fact that most of these surveys are conducted on or after discharge of the patient when the patient's attitudes must inevitably be influenced by the halo-effect that they are cured. Significantly different results may be obtained if these surveys were conducted within the first twelve hours of admission to hospital when the trauma of the admission rituals are still fresh in their minds.

Institutionalised expectations

However, Parsons (1964) asks the pertinent question: isn't 'being sick' simply a state of fact, a 'condition' and not a social role at all? But, conceding that things are never quite as simple as they seem, holds that the 'test is the existence of a set of institutionalised expectations and the corresponding sentiments and sanctions'.

He identifies four aspects of the institutionalised expectation system relative to the sick role.

The first is the exemption from the responsibilities of the individual's normal social role which is legitimated by relatives and the doctor. Avoiding the obligations of one's normal social role such as not working is both an obligation and a right for the sick person.

The second is the institutionalised definition that the sick person cannot recover by his own personal decision or will. Illness is a bridge to the acceptance of 'help' in which the 'condition' and not the 'attitude' of the patient must be changed by 'being taken care of'.

The third element is the definition of 'being ill' as an undesirable state for the individual and the implicit obligation to 'get well'.

The final element is the obligation of the sick individual to seek technically competent help from a doctor 'in proportion to the severity of the condition, of course' and to co-operate in the process of trying to get better.

After a discussion of the variations, to a greater or lesser extent, of these elements in various health care situations in medical practice, Parsons concludes that 'the basic problems of the role of the patient himself are shared by the others in his personal circle with whom the physician comes into contact in his practice. Sometimes the role of these others is to facilitate the work of the physician very significantly. But it would be rash to assert that this was true very much more often than the reverse'.

SOCIOCULTURAL RESPONSES TO THE PATIENT

The sociocultural responses that may contribute to the emotional-organic responses of the patient are considered by Strauss (1966) and he cites the characteristic responses of an individual who suffers a heart attack in the street.

The first response is to call the police and an ambulance, which invariably arrives with 'sirens ringing and frequently the manner of emergency pesonnel bubbles with crisis'.

The effects of these is usually not considered, Strauss argues, for, in our culture, the sound of the siren may incite fear or excitement and an ambulance may be a symbol of death. In any case, he holds, transportation to hospital in a private car may have a less harmful emotional impact on the individual, yet invariably he is transported by ambulance.

On arrival at the hospital, the patient, he adds, is subjected to a new kind of trauma, that of 'role-stripping'. All his symbols of personal identification are stripped off him. He finds himself dressed in strange clothes in a strange bed in a strange place surrounded by a number of strange faces.

The significance of particular illnesses to patients is determined to some extent, Strauss argues, by the patient's pre-existing beliefs and concepts which may lead him to view his illness with 'undue optimism or equally unwarranted graveness', affected by the excessive exposure to the mass media including the 'propaganda of voluntary health organisations'; he will have been asked to look for 'warning signs' and, as yet, research has not fully demonstrated whether this is effective in terms of prevention or whether it increases anxiety. It has however been tentatively suggested by reports from the Health Education Council that although their kind of propaganda intensifies awareness of symptoms it tends to cause undue anxieties without encouraging the affected individuals to seek help and treatment.

In hospital, most patients share rooms but, as Strauss points out, much could be done if thought were given to the grouping of patients to minimise irritability and trauma and maximise compatibility. Nothing is known, for example, of the effects of a group of patients suffering from myocardial infarction sharing the same room. 'Is there not a risk', he asks, 'should one patient experience crisis or death, the trauma of such a situation might invoke deep anxiety or even prove fatal to the other patient?'.

Citing a study relating to the planning of progressive care for hospital patients, he indicates that the average hospital patient may come into contact with as many as seventeen different people in a single day. That in itself, he holds, may impose some emotional strain but, where there is emphasis in the hospital on moving patients from one area to another area in response to administrative requirements, the patient may be required to relate to a new team of ten to seventeen new faces with each move.

In the management of patients suffering from myocardial infarction, he concludes that 'it may well be advisable to consider the impact of this complex system of interpersonal relationships and to make some provision for simplifying the network of personnel assigned for the patient's needs'. A conclusion that could be generalised, in my view, in the interests of all hospital patients.

Stress may also be minimised, he holds, during the 'role-stripping' phase by providing objects and people who signify sensitivity to the patient. 'The use of one's own pyjamas, the presence of familiar objects of clothing, or a favourite knick-knack and the knowledge that dear ones are nearby, can all be important in the planning of comprehensive care'.

And, as there is always a great danger that a syndrome of over-dependency may occur, great prudence is necessary during the rehabilitation phases of care so that whilst the patient is discouraged from overdoing things, he will, at the same time, be encouraged to do as much as he can for himself.

THE DEPENDENCY SYNDROME

The inherent dangers of the dependency syndrome for the patient have been well documented by Miller and Gwynne (1972) in their report of a study carried out in a number of institutions caring for physically handicapped individuals.

All human beings in hospitals and institutions have basic needs for physical resources such as accommodation, food, adequate medical supplies and so on and for human resources such as caring, catering and cleaning.

Inmates in institutions (and patients in hospital) in their dependent roles are the through-put of the psycho-physical dependence system created by the psycho-social and physical needs discussed above. These needs are met, in the analysis of Miller and Gwynne, by 'many sub-systems of activity'. For example, 'the input may be an inmate needing a bath, the conversion process consists of bathing him or helping him to bath himself, and the output is a clean inmate'.

Difficulties arise however if the assumption is made that 'this system is coterminous with the institution as a whole'.

As cripples are admitted to institutions because they are unable to fend for themselves, it is often inferred by the staff that the institution exists only to satisfy their dependent needs, Miller and Gwynne find. This produces what they conceptualise as the 'warehousing model' in which 'the individual as an independent being has no room for existence'. Apathy and listlessness are evidenced in a warehousing situation, they hold, due to the fact that once an inmate has been processed through one of the dependence sub-systems, there is no other role in another system into which he can be put. Once he has been converted from an inmate needing a bath to one who has been bathed, he can only wait to become the input of a further dependence sub-system, through which he will be dressed and fed and dosed and given occupational therapy and put to bed and so on.

Now this study has application for the nurse working in acute areas as well, for the warehousing model with its norm of 'dependency' was very closely correlated with having a high percentage of trained nurses on the staff of the institution. That there is something inherent in the make-up of the role of the nurse that fosters this dependency is indicated in the conclusion that the warehousing model represents an attempt to translate the model of the hospital into the setting of a residential institution. They do not challenge the underlying assumption that this model is 'appropriate' to the hospital and hold that in hospital the patient's dependency role is a means towards an end of restoring the patient to normal health in the world. As the only 'output' from an institution is as a corpse, it is argued that nursing skills are redirected from the task of curing to that of postponing death in the institution.

Without debating their particular perspective on the role of the nurse it is, however, pertinent to cite another finding from their study. In those institutions which employed mostly *untrained* staff, inmates were more likely to be provided with an opportunity for developing their capacities and abilities as independent individuals. The norm of these institutions is *achievement*.

It could be argued therefore that professional preparation for nurses is dysfunctional in some respects, particularly if reponsibilities for rehabilitation, the restoration to health and working capacity of a person incapacitated by mental or physical disease or injury, is accepted as part of the nurses' role. For rehabilitation, if it is to be really effective, must start from the moment an individual first becomes a patient.

DEPERSONALISATION

The depersonalisation effects on long-term handicapped and chronically sick patients of the dependency syndrome can be likened to the effects on slaves in North America as described by Elkins (1963).

In North America, the stereotype of the African slave as a docile, irresponsible 'Sambo' almost became internalised by the slaves over time as a personality-type entailing him being 'dependent for guidance and direction even to the procurement of his most indispensable necessities. Apart from this protection he has the helplessness of a child without foresight, without faculty of contrivance, without thrift of any kind'. Accommodating to the role of slave, Elkins shows, led to the slave idealising the situation so that he identified with it and took it into his personality. Sometimes, that which at first is feared and resented is finally loved. Similar processes occurred in prisoners who were sent to concentration camps by the Nazis in World War II. The SS men, Elkins holds, actually became father symbols as the prisoners gradually became 'reduced to complete and childish dependence upon their masters'. The camp in effect became 'a kind of grotesque patriarchy'.

In *Asylums*, Goffman (1968) has vividly described the insidious and relentless phenomena of 'total institution' and the processes of depersonalisation. He supports his findings by citing from the literature about army units, nunneries, schools, ships, prisons, and in particular, mental hospitals. In order to survive in the setting of a 'total institution' mental hospital, which strips the patient of the symbols of his individual identity, patients learn patterns of subservient behaviour which reflect and indeed reinforce the overwhelming power of the staff.

The mental patients in such an institution may have to take on permanently the depersonalised role that is demanded of him. These patients are thought to be more mentally afflicted by their condition than they really are in order to justify that the physical (custodial) care is all that is needed. And Goffman shows that such beliefs tend to have the character of self-fulfilling prophecy.

'The moral career of the mental patient has unique interest, however; it can illustrate the possibility that in casting off the raiments of the old self—or in having this cover torn away—the person need not seek a new robe and a new audience before which to cower. Instead he can learn, at least for a time, to practise before all groups the amoral arts of shamelessness'.

Barton (1959) popularised the term 'institutional neurosis' to describe the apathy listlessness and loss of motivation which, he claims, characterises many patients in long-stay hospitals. He holds that this condition is caused by the impersonal way in which long-stay hospital environments tend to deprive people of their sense of personal identity. But it is true that other psychiatrists have claimed that the behaviour which Barton attributes to the environment of the long-stay hospital may well be a symptom of chronic schizophrenia.

However, Mittler (1966) holds that during the movement from custodial to therapeutic regimes in mental hospitals it began to be appreciated that some of the violence and bizarre mannerisms that had previously been regarded as part of mental illness may be due to the environment of the hospital and to the way the patients had been treated in the past. 'Many people were surprised to discover that when the ward doors were unlocked no escapes or outbursts of violence occurred'.

It is, in fact, contended from time to time that the 'medical model' is an inappropriate model for the psychiatric patient. 'By some accident of history', Brewer (1974) contends, 'certain types of socially unacceptable behaviour and almost all types of individually unacceptable misery' became regarded as the preserve of medical men who naturally employ the concepts of medical men such as 'sickness' and the methods of medical men—that is 'treatments'.

Words like sickness and illness, Brewer points out, imply—to patients and doctors alike—that the patient is a victim of a process over which he has no control. Parsons' (1966) analysis supports this view.

'To be "sick" is to be passive, and if treatment is unsuccessful, the fault lies with the doctor but never with the patient'. Brewer argues that this 'medical model' way of thinking is still very much prevalent in the whole practice of psychiatry, which has resulted, he argues, in illogical and bad medical practice. Unhappy people are labelled as suffering from 'depressive illness' with the inevitable prescription of antidepressants. 'Numerous surveys show' that the mainstay of psychiatric treatment, especially in general practice, is 'medication and/or ECT'.

He concedes however that many psychiatrists recognise the relevance of environmental manipulation. But in doing so, Brewer contends, 'they fail to realise that what they try to achieve by psychotherapy may be entirely cancelled out by pharmacotherapy, since the former implies the patient is responsible for his own actions while the latter implies that he is not'. In fact, in practice,

Brewer finds that training of psychiatrists in the kinds of psychotherapy which could be of value in the care of psychiatric patients 'is almost non-existent'.

The fate of the patient in the general hospital ward who does not comply with the norms perceived by nurses to be appropriate to the role of patient has also been documented by Bowker (1973) who indicates that both social and physical santions can be directed against the unpopular patient. Not only do the nurses avoid social contact with him but they tend also to ensure, albeit subconsciously, that his bed position in the ward is in an appropriate place so as to enable the nurse to side-track him unobtrusively. And the irrationality of some of the traditional and barbaric practices to which the surgical patient can be submitted, such as being starved for 12 hours before surgery, have been highlighted and certain myths exploded in that respect by another study conducted by Smith (1972) among surgical patients.

Hayward (1975) has investigated the reactions of patients to pain and anxiety and finds that giving patients full information about their operations helps to allay their fears and also helps to reduce post-operative pain. Adequate pre-operative discussion with the patient also makes the post-operative phase easier for him.

A number of patients expressed their fears and, typically, could find out very little about what was happening to them, illustrated by one patient thus:

'I asked a nurse who said: "Don't you worry your head about all that. Just lie down and try to get to sleep". I think it was kindly meant, but it made me feel worse rather than better.'

There is some indication that ward sisters spend very little time in contact with patients, Hayward says, and he concedes that a drastic reorganisation of the system of hospital care would be necessary to allow ward sisters to spend half an hour talking to each patient who is admitted for surgery. This could only come about, he argues, by support from the 'highest levels of nursing management'.

Hayward also argues that it should not always be assumed that doctors and nurses always know what is best for the patient. The patient should be encouraged to participate in his own welfare, he holds. 'A surgical operation is a joint venture with the patient's welfare as the ultimate objective. Surely it is right that, wherever possible, the patient should participate in this venture and that he should be given enough information to anticipate events intelligently.' Who can disagree?

Conclusion

Throughout the first half of the twentieth century nurses and their colleagues worked in 'a compact hospital-based closed shop' Hector (1972) points out, where each health care worker had a well-established role.

The 'doctor was not only a practitioner but a revered Shaman; the nurse a ministering angel. Anauran Bevan, when Minister of Health, was recorded as saying that a nurse not working at the bedside was not a real nurse'.

As she rightly points out, such a restricted viewpoint is not possible today, for people often come into hospital for the cure of a condition, only to be returned to the community with different problems. Problems concerned with employment, finance, housing, status, transport, and so on. But problems that need care.

Corrective surgery on babies cuffering from spina bifida, for example, is now possible but, she reminds us, entails considering a number of consequences, not only for the child himself and his family but also for society at large and its community health and social services.

Increasingly complex demands are and will continue to be made on the nurse 'not only through scientific advance, but through more sophisticated expectations of colleagues and clients', she concludes.

If professionalisation of the nursing students is a socialisation process as is argued above then it follows that the nursing student needs time to internalise the appropriate systems of beliefs and attitudes; she needs time to identify with appropriate trained-nurse role models and needs time to build up relationships.

Is a 12-weeks maximum period of allocation of nursing students to clinical units sufficient time for all this to take place?

Might this short period of allocation also intensify for the patient the trauma associated with the role-stripping process of hospital admission procedures, as he is likely to be subjected to a constant flow of unfamiliar and strange faces? Perhaps the allocation of nursing students to clinical units for six or twelve months might be more functional for both student training and patient care?

These are just some of the questions which a study of the sociology of nursing will pose. The answers are in the hands of those responsible for formulating nursing education and service policies. Sociology, of course, will not provide the answers but can help policy makers to make more rational and realistic decisions that relate to the real world of health care.

REFERENCES

Barton, R. (1959) *Institutional Neurosis*. Bristol: Wright.
Birch, J. (1975) *To Nurse or Not to Nurse*. London: Royal College of Nursing.
Bowker, F. (1973) *The Unpopular Patient*. London: Royal College of Nursing.
Bowman, G. (1967) *The Lamp and the Book*. London: Royal College of Nursing.
Brewer, C. (1974) Last year's model. *New Psychiatry*, 8th August.
Brown, R.G.S. & Stones, R.W.H. (1973) *The Male Nurse*. London: Bell.
Bryden, E.G.M. (1969) *Integrated Course of Nurse Education—Study of an Experiment*. Queen's Institute of District Nursing.
Cooley, C.H., Angell, R.C. & Carr, L.J. (1939) *Introduction to Sociology*. New York: Harper & Row.
Durkheim, E. (1964) *Division of Labour in Society*. London: Collier-Macmillan.
Elkins, S.M. (1963) *Slavery*. New York: Grosset & Dunlap.
Goffman, E. (1968) *Asylums*. Pelican.
Hanrahan, E. (1971) *Report on the Training of Student Nurses*. Dublin: Irish Matrons Association.
Hayward, J. (1975) *Information—A Prescription Against Pain*. London: Royal College of Nursing.
Hector, W. (1972) The role and preparation of the teacher. *Nursing Times*, 16 November.
Hubert, M. (1967) Four basic university courses. *Nursing Times*, 6 October.
Hull, M. (1971) The 'role' courses. In *Social Significance of Education*. Boston University School of Nursing.
Lamond, N. (1974) *Becoming a Nurse*. London: Royal College of Nursing.
MacGuire, J.M. (1968) The function of the 'set' in hospital controlled schemes of nurse training. *British Journal of Sociology*, September.
MacGuire, J.M. (1969) *Threshold to Nursing*. London: Bell.
McLemore, S.D. & Hill, R.J. (1966) 'Role changes and socialization in nursing'. In *A Sociological Framework for Patient Care*. ed. Folta, J.R. & Deck, E.S. Wiley.
Mead, M. (1966) *Coming of Age in Samoa*. Harmondsworth: Pelican.
Miller, E.J. & Gwynne, G.V. (1972) *A Life Apart*. London: Tavistock.
Mittler, P. (1966) *The Mental Health Services*. London: Fabian Society.
Moores, B. (1975) *Expectations of Nurses of the Mentally Handicapped to Patient Accomplishment*. University of Manchester Institute of Science and Technology.
Moores, B. (1975) *On the Nature and Incidence of Staff-Patient Interactions in Hospitals for the Mentally Handicapped*. UMIST.
Mumford, E. & Skipper, J.K. (1967) *Sociology in Hospital care*. New York: Harper and Row.
Norton, D. (1972) *By Accident or Design*. Edinburgh: Livingstone.
Parsons, T. (1966) *On Becoming a Patient*. (Folta and Deck 1966: opus cit).
Ruano, B.J. (1971) This I believe . . . About nurses innovating change. *Nursing Outlook*, June.
Smith, J.P. (1969) Basic nursing education in Scandinavia. *Nursing Miror*, 10 January.
Smith, J.P. (1969) Implementing nursing research findings. *Nursing Mirror*, 21 March.
Smith, J.P. (1973) Graduates and nursing. *Nursing Times*, 26 July.
Smith, J.P. (1974) Nursing in North America. *Nursing Mirror*, 28 November.
Smith, S. Hamilton (1972) *Nil by mouth*. London: Royal College of Nursing.

Sorokin, P.A. (1964) *Social and Cultural mobility*. Collier-Macmillan.
Strauss, R. (1966) *Sociocultural considerations in the care of patients*. (Folra and Deck 1966: opus cit).
Report of the Committee on Nursing (1972). London: HMSO.
Report of the Committee on Hospital Complaints Procedure. (1974) London: HMSO.
Report of the Survey on Teachers of Nursing. (1975) London: General Nursing Council for England And Wales.

5

Roles—patient and nurse

The sociological concept of role is closely allied to the concept of function. What you do affects what you are. If there is a clear understanding of the concept of role it is easier to understand human behaviour in social situations, as role is a pattern sequence of learned actions performed by an individual in society.

The concept of role is derived from the theatre where actors take on roles. Quite obviously in social situations individuals do not 'act' roles; they 'are' the roles. Roles are the behaviours prescribed for and expected of all persons who perform certain functions such as mother, father, doctor, nurse and patient. Role therefore informs the role bearer of the appropriate dress, duties, talk, obligations, privileges and rights. Most individuals in society have several roles; for example, one individual can be a mother, nurse and local councillor, and generally speaking this person will be able to switch roles quite regularly as the appropriate behaviour and attributes of these roles are prescribed. Roles have important functions in social life, as they minimise uncertainty and trauma. For example, if a nursing officer is visiting a medical ward it can be guaranteed that she will not start doing ballet dances down the middle of the ward under normal circumstances, as her role is to monitor and co-ordinate the nursing care in the unit she manages. Therefore other actions are more appropriate to the role of nursing officer and her staff can expect her to act out her role accordingly. Of course, some people are not always well cast in their roles; this depends on their primary personality traits being compatible with the role. For example, male nurses who consider nursing to be a woman's job would not be very well cast in the role of nurse.

Roles are always reciprocal, such as mother-son, nurse-patient, husband-wife, and are part of role sets. The roles of patient, doctor and nurse fit a total pattern and belong to a role set.

ROLE VARIATIONS

Role strain can occur when an individual has difficulty in meeting the role expectations. This is a very important concept to bear in mind particularly during times of organisational change in health care organisations. This is likely to occur, for example, in nursing officers if their managers try and orientate them towards a 'clinical' role when they preceive their role to be 'managerial'. Role strain, if it is permitted to persist can soon result in role incompatibility.

An individual suffering from role incompatability believes that other persons hold incompatible expectations about how he should perform a particular role and he will then do one of three things:

He will become a 'moralist' and carry on doing what he believes to be legitimate; he will become an 'expedient' and consider the unpleasant social sanctions that might be applied if he does not conform, and act as desired by the other person: he might become a 'moral expedient' and try to achieve a balance in the role between what he wants and what his manager wants.

Role conflict can occur if an individual is expected to play two roles that are competing or antagonistic, as might occur in a woman who is a mother and a district nursing officer, or who is a new bride and a student nurse on night duty.

Occasionally individuals may exhibit behaviour appropriate to a particular role without having the feelings or beliefs which go with that role and therefore play the role 'tongue-in-cheek'. This phenomenon is called role-distance and might occur, for example, in a dedicated ward sister who is asked to act as a tutor during teaching staff shortages or if she becomes a tutor purely as a means of obtaining more pay without having a desire to teach.

The influence of the concept of role

The concept of role powerfully influences social life. In Victorian

England, middle-class ladies frequently fainted if they became excited; maids rarely did, because there was no one to catch them! Because of the interdependence of roles, middle-class ladies who fainted were caught by middle-class gentlemen. These days, fainting is not perceived to be appropriate behaviour for women of any class.

A change in types (and roles) of 'mental illness' has also occurred in recent decades. In Freud's time, 'conversion hysteria' was common but is relatively rare today and has been replaced in incidence by 'schizophrenia'. There is some suggestion that role playing is a way of resolving personal conflicts and this is topical as there is much current discussion on the convergence of men's and women's roles in society.

STATUS

Closely associated with the concept of role is the concept of status. Status of a role tends to be higher if it has more rights than others and therefore status relates to the relative position of a role in a whole system of roles.

In the present British health care organisation a district administrator has higher status than a senior nursing officer; a district nursing officer has higher status than an assistant district administrator. The district administrator and district nursing officer being co-equals on the District Management Team have similar status and therefore have equal rights, and so on.

In organisations, status is usually documented in organisation line charts.

Relationships between people in different roles in a system of roles, as found, for example, in a hospital, are often referred to as 'superordination' and 'subordination' relationships which reflect higher and lower status respectively. The nursing officer can refer to staff nurses as 'my subordinates' and they, in turn, can refer to her as 'our superordinate' (or superior).

Role of patient

Being a patient involves accepting a state of dependency: 'Can I go to the bathroom, nurse?' This is a most difficult role for any individual, as his usual role behaviour is totally disrupted. Before his illness he was independent and may have been used to giving orders and to being in a position of superiority either as an employer or as a father (or mother). Sickness prevents him from fulfilling his usual role which can give rise to role conflict. As a patient he has to take instructions rather than give them: 'You should drink lots of fluid for the next few days'. He has to take on what he perceives to be a subordinate role to the nurses and doctors: 'Patients are not allowed to use the kitchens!'

The sick woman might be concerned because she is unable to carry out her role obligations of a mother. The sick man might be distressed because he is unable to carry out the role obligations of a father.

Disruption in role behaviour also occurs for relatives, which often tends to be overlooked. The child of a sick mother who is deprived of her care may have to relate differently to a friend or relative and the healthy mother of a sick infant may experience jealousy and resentment if she feels that the mother role is being taken over by her child's nurse.

Patients and their relatives need sensitive guidance during periods of temporary breakdown of their normal role patterns.

Escapism

Occasionally people take on the role of patient to escape from their role obligations. Illness is perceived by these patients as a great relief and means of escape from their day-to-day responsibilities. They can relax into the role of patient legitimately and expect others to care for them and they can demand services they would not normally expect to receive. The child who hates school, for example, might complain of nausea so that he can exchange the role of pupil for the role of patient. The woman who dislikes sexual activity might complain of headaches so that she can exchange the role of wife for the role of patient. During wartime numerous incidences of trigger-finger paralysis occur in young men on the battlefield so that they can exchange the role of soldier for the role of patient.

Sickness in those circumstances is also a means of securing a rest from the demand of role fulfilment. The conditions suffered by these patients are called psychosomatic, a term which emphasises the interrelationships between the mind and the body but, in view of the social influences on these conditions, a more appropriate term would be psycho-socio-somatic. Such patients, however, should not have their pain, distress and discomfort dismissed as being 'all in the mind'. Symptoms are felt by patients to the same degree whether the cause is physical, psychological or social and should be relieved irrespective of the cause. But quite obviously different patients will have very different needs to be met by the nurse and very different kinds of nursing programmes will therefore be required for their care.

Role of Nurse

There are a number of aspects of the nurse's role: The willingness to serve patients and clients, the acceptance of certain nursing codes and ethics, the ability to keep confidences, and so on. Some of these aspects are taught by teachers, others are absorbed by imitating experienced professional nurses such as ward sisters and nursing officers who are the nursing student's role-models. Gradually throughout the period of training, the nursing student learns to act like a trained nurse and learns to perform the role as defined for the nurse.

In a way the role is independent of the person who is the role holder. For example, if Mary Jones is a nurse, the role of nurse is independent of Mary Jones. Every nurse must act the role of nurse according to the prescribed and expected pattern whether the person is Mary Jones, John Brown or Alice White who, even though they might be and often are very different kinds of people, will generally carry out the functions of the role of nurse in a fairly standardised fashion. If that were not the case, chaos would reign in the average hospital unit or community health centre as neither health care colleagues or patients and clients would have any constant ideas of what kind of behaviour to expect from nurses.

There is another way of looking at the role of the nurse and that is by looking at the functions of the role. In task-orientated groups like nurses, two kinds of functions at least appear necessary if the group is to succeed and, in nursing, Barnard and Thomson (1970) identify these functions as the *instrumental* function or get-the-thing-done role and the *emotional-expressive* (sometimes called *affective*) function or keeping-the-people-willing-to-work role.

Citing the work of Schulman (1958), Barnard and Thompson indicate that these two functions have been analysed in respect to nursing as the *healer* and *mother-surrogate* roles. The healer role entails limited and impersonal contacts with patients and a more intellectual approach to nursing: this role is a curing role. The mother-surrogate role entails compassion, protection and tenderness for the patient and identification with him: this role is a caring role.

It is possible therefore that the role of the nurse can be perceived as either being that of a ministering angel or an efficient rational technician. This makes if difficult, however, to derive a consensual view on the role of the nurse and indeed there is some evidence to suggest that the roles of surgical and medical nurses are significantly different. The results of a study of medical and surgical nurses conducted by Lentz and Michaels (1959) consistently disclosed superior nurse-patient relationships in medical nurses and superior technical skills in surgical nurses.

ROLE CONFLICT FOR THE NURSE

The members of the nursing profession are particularly susceptible to role conflict by the very nature of their jobs and career development patterns. The nearer the nurse is to the patient the lower her status in the professional hierarchy. The more advanced and skilled nurses become, and therefore the more useful to the patient, the further they go from the patient when they seek career development as administrators of the nursing service and teachers of nursing.

This situation has created much discussion both in North America and in the United Kingdom. Unit managers have been introduced into a number of North American hospitals in an attempt to relieve nurses of non-nursing administrative duties. The unit manager relieves the head nurses in the unit of all non-nursing duties, makes social rounds of patients to deal with non-medical matters such as health insurance and oversees maintainence of equipment, orders and stores, and supervises ward clerks (Smith 1974).

There is some evidence that significant amounts of nurses' time have been saved by introducing unit managers, but not all of the time has been redirected to patient care as Jelinek *et al.* (1971) found after a study of unit management schemes in North American hospitals. Although they believe that the system provides an opportunity for a 'radical reconceptualisation of nursing', they found that the opportunity has not, so far, been fully grasped. 'For although the professional staff was relieved by selected non-professional activities, the major problem . . . was the absence of clear reorientation of the nurse practitioner . . . it is clear that the professional nurse has not taken full advantage of the opportunity . . .' Nevertheless, they expected some form of unit management to be found in most larger hospitals by the end of the seventies.

PERVASIVE IMAGERY OF BEDSIDE NURSING

As long as non-clinical career development for nurses persists, role conflict is likely to persist, Strauss (1966), argues because of the 'pervasive imagery of bedside nursing' which, he points out, 'persists despite great and increasing numbers of nurses who administrate or teach in schools of nursing'. He holds that:

'The persistence of this imagery has something to do with the reality but also with sacred aspects of the profession. Nurses are not so different from other professionals who idealise some cluster of esteemed activities supposedly embodying the very essence of their particular profession (lawyers litigate in courts of justice, physicians give medical care). Of course, not everyone in a profession engages in such characteristic professional actions. Inevitably such a great diversity of tasks are performed in the name of any profession that its different segments do not agree upon the full range of activities which the profession ought to encompass or exactly how its work should be organised. Nevertheless, certain traditional activities appear to tap such deeply embedded sentiments that although "not all of us" are engaged in the work which historically marked us off from every other profession, the work does remain truly ours.' The dilemma may well be a perennial one as indicated in the sentiments of Brown (1971) who considers it little short of scandalous that nurses are distracted from clinical involvement due, in her view, to planners rarely providing nurses with an opportunity for intellectual growth and professional advancement through progressively greater competence as clinical practitioners. 'The choices open to these nurses', she argues, 'have been to adjust to the system which probably results in decreasing motivation and competence, to drop out of nursing or to seek advancement via the administrative ladder', which leads, she argues, to 'the consequence that administration is likely to become top heavy and bureaucratic having removed all decision making from the level of direct patient care'.

Different perceptions of a role

The role of the nursing officer is new in the British nursing services and the discussion and debate that it has engendered are sociologically fascinating.

The *Report on Senior Nursing Staff Structure* (Salmon Report, 1966) describes the role of the nursing officer as a person who 'will have special knowledge of the techniques of the specialities in her unit' so that she can act as consultant to the charge nurse, and she will also be qualified by virtue of the training she has received in management to 'programme the work of the unit . . . there will remain with her the same kind of continuing responsibility for her unit as by tradition rested with the Matron . . . act as consultant in nursing practice . . . participate personally in training of nursing staff . . .'.

A review of a number of articles in nursing journals, written by nursing officers appointed after the Salmon Report recommendations were implemented, illustrates wide and varying opinions on the nursing officer's role. Franks (1970) believes that a completely new pattern of administration is evolving but concedes that it is not easy to describe the role of the nursing officer because of his involvement with personnel problems more than administrative procedures! But, in his view, it is 'becoming clear that units will tend to be specialist, and therefore the nursing officer needs to be an expert in the clinical aspects', and he concludes that the role of nursing officer is still evolving and only continued experiment will show exactly what responsibilities and duties nursing officers undertake.

Another nursing officer, Richardson (1970), considers the nursing officer's role to be 'unique in its many facets' and 'complex' and 'by its nature intangible'. After comparing the role with that of a middle manager in industrial organisations he concludes that it is difficult for the nursing officer to be 'seen to be successful' but believes that 'this is perhaps one of the greatest of all incentives'.

A former assistant matron, appointed to the post of nursing officer, argues that the nursing officer's role is 'a clinical role with an administrative content'.

Cheadle (1972), after observing a nursing officer at work for three weeks covering the full cycle of shifts, found that 36.1 per cent of the nursing officer's time was spent in the office because of hospital administrative commitments and only 14.9 per cent of his time was devoted to his own unit's patients and affairs.

An analysis of comments and questionnaires completed by 40 nursing officers (21 female, 19 male) working within the same nursing organisation (Smith, 1977) showed that only 3 per cent of all comments concerned clinical aspects of the role of the nursing officer, whereas 63 per cent of all comments concerned managerial aspects. 'There was a greater emphasis on the managerial aspects in the comments made by the male nursing officers.'

However, analysis of the completed questionnaires revealed that 62.5 per cent of the nursing officers considered clinical aspects to be the most important factor in their role, whereas only 10 per cent considered managerial aspects to be the most important factor. At first sight, these answers appear to conflict with the verbal comments. If Strauss (1966) is right about the 'pervasive imagery of bedside nursing', it could well be that the verbal comments are a more accurate illustration of the nursing officers' true perceptions of their role and that their written answers to the questionnaire are rationalisations.

The statement that 'the nursing officer's position is a stepping stone to promotion' was endorsed by 70 per cent of the respondents. If increasing numbers of nursing officers see their position as a stepping stone to further promotion, serious implications for patients care may arise, as there could well be little stable support for the charge nurse working at ward level, who as Bendall (1972) observed, 'is often young and inexperienced . . . (and) . . . quite unprepared for the demands made, for her training has been traditional and she has been taught to do rather than to think, and no one has seen fit to give her the necessary skills, though she often has the potential'.

THE DILEMMA IN CLARIFYING A ROLE

If the role of nursing officer is perceived so differently among the role bearers themselves it is obviously somewhat difficult to determine what the role really is or ought to be.

The dilemma was made manifest in growing concern expressed by large numbers of nurses in the 1960s and 1970s. There was a feeling that the role of the nurse needed clarifying, and a reorientation towards a clinically identifiable role was commended. Pressures resulted in the *Committee on Nursing* being set up by Richard Crossman, the Secretary of State for Social Services, with the brief:

'To review the role of the nurse and midwife in hospital and the community and the education and training required for that role.'

The Committee published its report in 1972 and among its many conclusions was that the nursing officer post is 'often a combined clinical/managerial post and there are now significant numbers of Nursing Officers carrying out jobs with considerable clinical content'. The report expresses unease about sharp distinctions between clinical, managerial and teaching responsibilities since, it holds, there are managerial and teaching elements in the role of all nurses and midwives.

Ambiguities about the nursing officer's role persist and this is demonstrated quite convincingly in a Scottish report—*Review of the Senior Nursing Staff Structure* (1975).

The report, which is based on research findings of a study conducted among over two thousand Scottish nurses, considers that the role of the nursing officer still needs further investigation and further considers that the ambiguity about the role may be due to role expectations not having been realised where the nursing officer manages a unit of mixed specialities.

A working group of members of the nursing and medical professions, convened in 1978 by the Royal College of Physicians, Edinburgh, concluded that the nursing officer occupies a difficult position and held that the role of the nursing officer is not yet that of the 'nurse consultant'. It was also noted that there appeared to be no formal provision for horizontal communication between the nursing officer and senior medical staff. It was felt that nursing officers were often unclear about their role and suffered from the lack of formal lines of communication with medical staff. 'Persistence of multi-unit systems in the larger teaching hospitals also creates barriers for nursing officers and in many areas medical staff are also unclear of her role.' The working group's report also states that the nursing officer 'has less opportunity to maintain clincal expertise' because of inadequate support from clerical, personnel and secretarial services, and the burdensome administrative responsibilities resulting from recent employment legislation.

THE HEALTH VISITOR, MIDWIFE AND OCCUPATIONAL HEALTH NURSE

A review of the literature on the role of the health visitor would demonstrate an equal divergence of opinion on this role. There appear to be three camps, one which sees health visiting as an extension of nursing, one which sees health visiting as specialised medicosocial work and one which considers health visiting to be a profession in its own right.

Functions of the role of the health visitor include prevention, health education, family planning, social counselling, primary care and so on, all of which have been given some support by the literature but as yet there seems to be no real consensus about what health visiting is, nor is any priority given to the various functions mentioned above.

Studies conducted by health visitors June Clark (1973) and Patricia B. Hobbs (1973) suggest that the training for the perceived role of health visitor does not particularly fit the health visitor practitioners for the roles in family care or health education and group teaching activities. There is some strong indication that many health visitors are forced into situations or have to initiate activities for which they have not been prepared properly. This suggests a conflict between the role of the health visitor as perceived by her educators and the actual role of the practising health visitor in the field.

Discussing how midwives and obstetricians view the role of the midwife, Walker (1976) notes the possibility of a midwife/obstetric nurse dichotomy. She maintains that although accepted definitions of the midwife imply that the midwife is trained to care for women during the normal process of childbirth and that her role is complementary to that of the obstetrician who is concerned primarily with the application of scientific knowledge to ensure the clinical well-being of mother and infant, the midwives' claim to be practitioners in their own right is rarely recognised in practice.

A similar dilemma exists for the British occupational health nurse. In discussing her role, Jarman (1978) states categorically that the occupational health nurse is not a doctor, but may on occasions be a safety worker, for example when giving advice on safety in the home. She argues that this is part of caring for the individual and rightfully the function of a nurse. She believes, however, that the occupational nurse 'will probably have great difficulty in establishing herself as an independent health practitioner and can expect great opposition if she tries to extend her role beyond the concept held by management, trade unions and doctors'.

The development of new roles for those who provide health care is tied inextricably to the social structure of the health care system and to the environment within which that system functions (Christman, 1979). The social structures, and consequently the roles in which people place or find themselves, often predicate their behaviour better than either their psychological traits or their training. In Christman's view, organisational arrangements exert a powerful influence on role behaviour. They may inhibit or encourage progressive activities, discourage or foster cooperation between the various role holders in the organisation, retard or promote continuity of effort and disrupt or facilitate communications within the organisation. The behaviour of nurses, physicians and others involved in health care is therefore directly affected by its organisation.

CLINICAL NURSE CONSULTANT: A NEW ROLE

Among the many bodies and individuals who submitted evidence to the Committee on Nursing was the Royal College of Nursing (RCN) which felt strongly that a new post of clinical nurse consultant should be created. In an attempt to have this concept endorsed by the members, the RCN Council, at the meeting of representatives from throughout the United Kingdom in 1971, proposed the following motion:

'That this meeting of the RCN representative body strongly supports the recommendations in the RCN evidence to the Committee on Nursing that an advanced clinical role for the nurse/midwife be identified by the creation of posts of nurse/midwife consultant.'

The minutes of the meeting record that in the course of a long discussion 'a number of speakers including members of the Ward and Departmental Committee, expressed reservations on the proposal and thought that the proposed new post would conflict with posts in the Salmon structure'. No vote was taken and, to the Council's dismay, the meeting successfully resolved to 'move to next business' without making a decision.

In 1971 two British nurses published opinions based on reviews of the literature on the role of clinical nurse consultant as developed over the previous 10 years in North America. They both differed in their views.

I myself concluded that: 'It is sobering to note that, even in the USA, there have been disagreements about the specialist's role expections by "significant others", namely hospital administrators, directors of nursing, physicians—and even by the role-bearers themselves'.

Juanita B. Rule, former director of education at the RCN, concluded that: 'It is true that one can select from the articles supporting evidence for one's own prejudices either for or against the role of clinical nurse specialist, but there is no doubt . . . that it is a fully professional role, the success of which depends on a willingness to give those with an original competence an unusual freedom to choose, to act and to innovate'.

At the RCN representatives' meeting in the following year (1972), the concept of the clinical nurse consultant was aired once more at great length and a resolution was proposed by representatives from Aberdeen and London:

'That this meeting of the RCN representative body request Council no longer to pursue the policy of introducing the role of clinical nurse consultant, as put forward in the RCN evidence, to the committee on nursing.' The motion was lost!

The *Report of the Committee on Nursing* (1972) gave no explicit endorsement to the role of clinical nurse consultant which probably illustrates the very great difficulties inherent in any attempt to be explicit about the complexities of any nursing role. But these difficulties are universal and even an international body such as the International Council of Nurses has difficulty when it attempts from time to time to produce a definition of the role of the nurse which will be acceptable to all the national organisations in membership.

The Royal Commission on the National Health Service (1979) argues 'that the nursing officer should have a satisfying role with combined professional, administrative, and personnel functions'. However, so far, her professional functions of acting as consultant in nursing practice, developing new ideas and methods, and teaching have emerged in only a few places. Among a number of reasons for this, the Commission indicated that the management content of her role is often so demanding that little time is left for clinical involvement and that the training for nursing officers has often emphasised the management role to the exclusion of preparation for an advanced clinical role. The Commission also points out that 'there is a real difficulty for grades above ward sister acting as consultants and advisers on clinical care if they do not take responsibility for the care of individual patients'.

In September 1979, shortly after the publication of this report, the Royal College of Nursing, in its submission to the Standing Committee on Pay Comparability, supported the case for a nurse consultant/specialist, thereby implicitly accepting that not all nursing officers' roles are clinical roles. 'Promotion to the post of ward sister/charge nurse necessitates the acquisition of many varied skills relating to the management and delivery of patient care, but it is for many nurses the final opportunity for promotion and salary advancement in the clinical field . . . further promotion, except to the post of nursing officer in a functional unit, will require the nurse to move away from direct patient care.'

In 1979, the Royal College of Nursing argued once more that it is 'essential that the nurse practitioner should be able to progress to a post of consultant/specialist in a particular branch of nursing, no longer retaining responsibility for an individual ward, department or district, but instead being recognised as an expert on specialist nursing care, and being consulted by nursing colleagues and those other health care practitioners who are directly involved in various aspects of the care of patients and clients in order to assist in the resolution of particular nursing problems'.

A problem shared

Two American nurses, Boucher and Bruce (1973), in a rigorously conducted study, have attempted to assess the perceptions and valuations of nurse educators, nurse clinicians, nurse administators and nurse practitioners of the role of the clinical nurse specialist. Their findings illustrate further the difficulties inherent in the concept of role.

The educator group perceived the clinical nurse specialist as a researcher-educator, with little involvement as a change agent but their valuations of the role were different to their perceptions.

The clinical nursing specialist group perceived their role exactly in the same way as the educators but disagreed with the educator's valuations.

The nursing administrators group perceived the specialist as an educator-researcher with practitioner expertise, with little involvement as a change agent.

Educators and nursing administrators completely agreed in their valuations of the specialist role.

The nursing practitioners group perceived the specialist as an educator-researcher with change agent competencies but little expert practitioner involvement. This group differed quite significantly to the other three groups' valuations of the specialist role.

The only complete agreement reached by all groups was that they all perceived and evaluated the clinical nursing specialist as a non-administrator.

The results of the perception— valuation comparisons are summarised in Table 5.1.

Table 5.1 Perception–Valuation comparisons (after Boucher and Bruce, 1973)

Groups	*Comparison*	*Perception of Role: Valuation of Functions*
Educators		
	Perception	Researcher–Educator–Practitioner–Change Agent
	Valuation	Educator–Practitioner–Researcher–Change Agent
Clinicians		
	Perception	Researcher–Educator–Practitioner–Change Agent
	Valuation	Educator–Practitioner–Change Agent–Researcher
Administrators		
	Perception	Educator–Researcher–Practitioner–Change Agent
	Valuation	Educator–Practitioner–Researcher–Change Agent
Practitioners		
	Perception	Educator–Researcher–Change Agent–Practitioner
	Valuation	Change Agent–Educator–Practitioner–Researcher

More recently Ruth and Partridge (1978) have indicated that the problems in Master's programmes in American schools of nursing are compounded by the divergence of opinion among community health nurses about their role. As a result profound problems threaten the viability of community health nursing as a specialty within nursing and public health in North America. They point out that even the terms 'community health nursing' and 'public health nursing' can denote a certain bias or perspective. They suggest that the most important problem is the fundamental division in philosophy and perspectives among community health nurses themselves. 'These differences are so basic as to keep us from agreeing on substance and scope of our speciality, as well as on how to prepare advanced practitioners for the field.'

THE ROLE OF NURSE PUT IN PERSPECTIVE

The problem of clarifying the role of the nurse, clearly associated with the ambiguity of needs and goals in nursing is fraught with difficulty, but not insurmountable as Professor Margaret Scott Wright (1973) observes:

'The one overall pompous and rather pious objective which is always on the lips of nurses and midwives, but which as a generality is rather meaningless, is their concern with the provision of good and better nursing care. It sounds excellent but what does it mean? . . The plain and awkward truth is that almost nothing is known about it in a profession that has had neither the opportunity nor the inclination to pursue it scientifically . . . First, the answers will need a scientific research basis; and secondly, this macroscopic goal of good nursing care must be broken down into meaningful small objectives which have some relevance to the work of groups of nurses and midwives in different care categories of the profession.'

The implication of those words is that the nursing profession and its members must search for and accept the uniqueness of a number of nursing roles which will vary according to the unique situation in which the nurse is caring for each unique patient or client in the process of promoting their complete mental, physical and social wellbeing.

What could be a 'crisis of identity' was put succinctly into perspective by Rule (1974) in concluding *The Nursing Lecture 1974* at the Royal College of Nursing's Annual General Meeting in London:

'Nevertheless, the future of nursing would seem more promising than it has ever been in terms of recognition of its contribution to those that need us; in terms of doing a more adequate job because we are adapting to changed circumstances, and thereby helping to reduce the sum total of misery and pain, by bringing our skill, comfort and support where it is needed.'

'It does not seem to me to matter whether a nurse chooses to work in intensive care, in industry, the home, the clinic or the operating theatre, as manager, teacher or practitioner. To do all those things she needs to have a broad comprehensive basis of education on which her selected speciality is grafted, and in which she seeks her excellence.'

REFERENCES

Barnard, J. & Thomson L.F. (1970) *Sociology: Nurses and their Patients in a Modern Society*. Mosby.

Boucher, R.J. & Bruce, S.J. (1973) Similarities and differences in perception and valuation of functions of the role of the clinical nursing specialist. Unpublished paper, Boston University, School of Nursing.

Brown, E.L. (1971) *Nursing Reconsidered, Part 2*. Philadelphia: Lippincott.

Cheadle, J. (1972) The work of a nursing officer. *Nursing Mirror*, 18 August.

Christman L. (1979) New roles for personnel: nurses and physician extenders. *Bulletin of the New York Academy of Medicine*. **55,** 37–40.

Clark, J. (1973) *A Family Visitor*. London: Royal College of Nursing.

Franks, G. (1970) A nursing officer's view of 'Salmon'. *British Hospital Journal and Social Science Review*, 17th July.

Hobbs, P. (1973) *Aptitude or Environment: a Study of the Group Teaching Activities of Health Visitors*. London: Royal College of Nursing.

Jarman, B.M. (1978) The extending role of the British occupational health nurse. *Journal of Advanced Nursing*, **3,** 189–198.

Jelinek, R.C. (1971) *SUM: An Organisational Approach to Improved Patient Care*. Kellog Foundation.

Lentz, E.M. & Michaels, R.G. (1959) Comparisons between medical and surgical nurses. *Nursing Research, New York*, Autumn.

Richardson, D.K. (1970) Our man in the field. Salmon structure: No 7. *Nursing Mirror*, 4 September.

Royal College of Nursing (1979) *Submission to the Standing Commission on Pay Comparability*. London: Royal College of Nursing.

Royal College of Physicians (1978) *Cooperation between Medical and other Health Professions*. Royal College of Physicians, Edinburgh.

Rule, J.B. (1971) Book Review of *The clinical nurse specialist*. *Nursing Times*, 24 June.

Rule J.B. (1974) *A Crisis of Identity*. London: Royal College of Nursing.

Ruth, M.V. & Partridge, K.B. (1978) Differences in perception of education and practice. *Nursing Outlook*, October, 622–628.

Schulman, S. (1958) Basic functional roles in nursing: mother surrogate and healer. In *Patients, Physicians and Illness* by J.E. Gartly. Free Press of Glencoe.

Scott Wright, M. (1973) Needs and goals in nursing. *District Nursing*, January.

Smith, J.P (1971) Clinical nurse consultants: A case for caution? *Nursing Times*, 24 June.

Smith, J.P. (1977) The unit nursing officer: manager of nursing care. *Journal of Advanced Nursing*, **2,** 571–588.

Strauss, A. (1966) The Structure and Ideology of American Nursing. In *The Nursing Profession: Five Sociological Essays*, ed. Davis, F. New York: Witney.

Walker, J.F. (1976) Midwife or obstetric nurse? *Journal of Advanced Nursing*, **1,** 129–138.

Report of the Committee on Senior Nursing Staff Structure (HMSO, 1966)

Report of the Committee on Nursing (HMSO, 1972)

Review of the Senior Nursing Staff Structure (Scottish Home and Health Department, 1975)

Minutes of the Royal College of Nursing's Representatives Body Meetings (1971 and 1972)

6

The nursing profession

'The real origins of nursing are lost in the mists of time', as Dr. Dorothy Hall (1980), regional nurse for Europe, World Health Organisation, pointed out in the fifth Battersea Memorial Lecture. The discipline known as nursing, she said, results from the evolution within society of a fundamental human activity—the activity of caring: 'nursing arises out of the needs of all persons for succour, comfort, care and support in varying states of health'. Thus, nursing is part of the basic fabric of all societies and it possesses a form and life which is 'independent of any group of professionals which a society may generate in an endeavour to develop and systematise it'.

No matter at what level, whether local, regional, national or international, Dr. Hall stresses that organised nursing can only be understood, developed and interpreted in terms of its position within the situation existing at any one time in society. Therefore, she contends, if nurses wish to influence the future, they must come to grips with its possible shape and structure. They must find attractive ways of sustaining the needs of the present while at the same time making plans for the future and possible adjustments to the nurse's role.

THE MARKS OF A PROFESSION

All nurses, their colleagues and patients tend to speak regularly, and without giving much thought to the matter, about the nursing profession. They do not have too much concern as to whether or not nursing has any right to be called a profession at all. The topics of profession, semi-profession and pseudo-profession have commanded the attention of numerous writers and it is quite difficult to determine any particular consensus about what a profession really is or ought to be. Definitions range from vague: 'The term profession . . . clearly stands for something. That something is a complex of characteristics' (Carr-Saunders and Wilson, 1964) to the erudite: 'The word profession connotes for most people a foundation of science and a motive of service. That is, a profession is said to rest on the basis of a proved body of knowledge, and such knowledge is supposed to be used in the service of others rather than merely for one's own purposes.' (Mary Parker Follett 1965).

After a fairly rigorous review of the literature Catherine M. Hall (1973), General Secretary of the Royal College of Nursing, opted for the following main characteristics of a profession which are as useful as any as a basis for discussion.

A profession, in her view:

1. provides a service to society, involving specialised knowledge and skills
2. possesses a unique body of knowledge which the profession constantly seeks to extend in order to improve the service it provides
3. educates its own practitioners
4. sets its own standards
5. adapts its services to meet changing needs
6. accepts responsibility for safeguarding the clients it services
7. strives to make economical use of its practitioners
8. promotes the welfare and wellbeing of its practitioners and safeguards their interests
9. is motivated more by its commitment to the service it provides than by considerations of economic gain
10. adheres to a code of conduct based on ethical principles
11. unites for strength in achieving its larger purposes
12. is self governing.

It might be more difficult to apply these criteria to the nursing profession than to other professions such as medicine or law, but doctors and lawyers have practised as independent practitioners for a long, long time and nursing is relatively young in professional age. However, on the whole, people generally speak about the nursing 'profession' and the *Report of the Committee on Nursing* (Briggs Report 1972), it can be claimed, describes nursing as the 'major caring profession'.

THE ROLE OF THE PROFESSIONAL ASSOCIATION

The significant and important role of the United Kingdom's major professional organisation for nurses, The Royal College of Nursing of the United Kingdom, during the first 60 years of its existence (1916–1976) has been documented by Simpson (1977). She concludes that the College has contributed to the development of nursing in two ways: On the one hand, it has provided opportunities for the professional growth of individual members through educational, library and research facilities, and on the other hand, members of the Royal College of Nursing have been able to contribute to the development of the profession of nursing itself. 'A nursing voice has been able to speak on patient needs and clinical practice, on education and the National Health Service structure, salaries and conditions of work and on a thousand other matters.'

Hall (1973), whilst conceding the lack of consistency in accepting that nursing does not fully meet the criteria to be called a profession, submits that 'nursing can make this claim because it reflects certain of the characteristics of a profession to a very high degree and, in respect of the others, it can be seen to be evolving'. She admits, however, that nursing is subject to a variety of external controls but these controls can be modified, she holds, by the influence of a professional association. These controls are identified as the *primary* controls of professional education and qualification, registration and legal definitions, government policies, employment policies, the organisation and management of nursing services, the development of the unique body of knowledge, and the *secondary* controls of relationships with the medical profession, other professions, economic resources, manpower constraints, consumer needs and demands, and supporting services.

The professional association, she contends, influences these controls in a variety of ways:

1. By setting as a primary objective the provision for nursing

education in professionally controlled schools of nursing where they do not exist. They do exist in the United Kingdom.

2. By pressing for registration of qualified practitioners (where it does not exist) to enhance professional standing and safeguard the public. In the United Kingdom, statutory bodies exist for this purpose. (They were all united together by the creation, in 1980 of the United Kingdom Central Council for Nursing, Midwifery and Health Visiting. Miss Hall was appointed its first chairman).

3. By achieving a position whereby the professional association can, at will, make representations to government on any matter concerning the nursing profession. The largest organised body of nurses in the United Kingdom—the Royal College of Nursing—possesses this long-established right.

4. By helping to determine employment policies relating to, *inter alia*, salaries, conditions of service, protection of nursing employees. The Royal College of Nursing has the largest number of representatives on the Whitley Council negotiating body and is therefore in a position of maximum influence on these matters.

5. By making strenuous efforts to ensure that where it is not the case, the nursing services are organised and managed by nurses and that adequate preparation for managerial roles is available. The nursing services in the United Kingdom are in fact organised and managed by nurse managers who since the introduction of the Integrated National Health Service in 1974 have been afforded an exciting opportunity for developing a truly executive role. And the average British ward sister has a long established autonomous role in her clinical domain.

It could be argued therefore that British nursing has a professional status unique in the world, including North America, where in spite of the very high levels of basic and post-basic nursing education, which inevitably must foster high levels of professional aspiration, 'it is doubtful if these high aspirations can ever be met as the North American head nurse appears to have none of the clinical autonomy of the British ward sister, nor has the North American director of nursing any of the executive authority of the British district nursing officer' (Smith 1974). The Royal College of Nursing representatives on official government committees and working parties have undoubtedly influenced the government policies from which these new roles have been developed and have, over the years, pioneered advanced education courses for ward sisters and nursing service managers as well as representing them nationally and internationally.

6. By promoting research and investigations and research-mindedness to develop a body of knowledge. The Royal College of Nursing pioneered nursing care research in the United Kingdom in a specially funded research unit and sponsored twelve studies all designed to throw light on different aspects of nursing care in general hospital wards. These studies have made significant contributions to the body of knowledge and have also produced thirty-five research tools for the use of further researchers. Officers and members of the college have also collaborated with some eminent nurses from overseas to pioneer a bi-monthly *Journal of Advanced Nursing* which solicits scholarly original papers from nurses, *inter alia,* to help develop further the body of nursing knowledge and to share this knowledge internationally. But as yet nursing only has an embryonic body of knowledge.

The professional association can also influence external contacts by doing as much as possible to achieve desirable relationships at national level by establishing contact with medical professional associations. Nursing and medicine are interdependent and therefore patients will benefit more fully from health care developments only if the two professions advance together in partnership. 'The Royal College of Nursing has a long-established link with the British Medical Association which has resulted, over the years, in a marked change in attitude of the medical profession', Hall contends and goes on to demonstrate how the professional association can effectively modify the other secondary external controls mentioned above.

It could be argued therefore that development of professional status is closely correlated with the development of an appropriate professional organisation and certainly this thesis will find some support if comparison is made between nursing and other new professions such as teaching, social work and paramedical professions like physiotherapy, radiography and chiropody. Nursing as a profession might appear to lag behind in status compared to the traditional professions of the law, the church and medicine but it is more mature as a profession than others.

Nursing therefore has already established the right to be called a profession to a great extent. A heartening note of endorsement is recorded by Margaret Scott Wright (1974), first professor of nursing studies in the University of Edinburgh (now dean of the faculty of nursing, University of Calgary, Canada), who feels that because nurses implemented the recommendations of the *Report of the Committee on Senior Nursing Staff Structure* (1966) so quickly, they were well prepared to take their places as fully professional equal members in new multi-disciplinary management teams and that these new administrative posts are vital for safeguarding the expanding role and function of nurses in all sectors of the profession. And when the winds of change blowing through society and profession settle, she holds that no profession will be in a stronger position to face up to current changes and the future demands of health care than nursing. Such confidence in the competence of the members of the nursing profession surely implies professionalism.

But Professor Scott Wright urges the importance of the acquisition of another attribute by members of the nursing profession: 'For nursing to meet all its obligations to the future, there is an important factor which must be added to our thinking and activity—political-mindedness (with a small "p") . . . What is needed is a new sense of strategy and political-mindedness befitting a profession of such social importance as nursing.'

Political consciousness as an essential attribute of the professional nurse has been described by Schröck (1977) as an illusion, and possibly a dangerous one if nurses persist in the belief that nursing as a profession is unpolitical activity. She contends that nurses need to develop critical abilities in their understanding and analysis of the socioeconomic and political background to the health care services which employ them. She also points out that they are a potentially powerful group of health care workers.

The welfare state, social thought and planning, and politics of health care are used by Schröck as examples to demonstrate the kind of critical understanding which nurses need to acquire in order to deal with some of the fundamental assumptions that directly or indirectly influence their work. Even though nurses may prefer to think of health care as something outside politics, associating politics with partisanship, fighting for power, and inequality, 'such strongly held mistaken belief must mitigate against the vital realisation that health care without politics is simply not possible' (Schröck).

Professional education

Those responsible for nursing education carry a special responsibility as they must ensure that the nursing student is sufficiently orientated and motivated to aspire to the status of being a professional nurse, succinctly described by Kelly (1968) as a nurse who 'is motivated by a desire to help others; she constantly seeks new knowledge and ways to improve her nursing services; and she is keenly aware of nursing as an essential service to society. She doesn't just work at nursing she *is* a nurse—a professional nurse'.

What should the professional educational programme therefore contain? This question is often asked and often answered—in different ways—by students of nursing curriculum. But recently, both question and answer have been discussed in some detail by Christine Chapman, director of advanced nursing studies in the University of Wales (1974), who cites a definition of nursing, attributed to Lisbeth Hockey of the University of Edinburgh, as 'the act of applying nursing science, nursing science being a unique mix of other sciences with the uniqueness lying in the mix', but hastily adds a plea for more research to identify the breadth and depth required of these 'other sciences'. However she commends a 'mix' in basic nursing education programmes of behavioural, biological and medical sciences; management, nursing and educational theories; and manual skills.

And she contends that 'for all students, education must allow the development of the individual and this should be encouraged by allowing particular interests or skills to be preserved and developed . . . This may result in a reappraisal of many of our sacred cows but is the only way we can ensure a healthy profession able to meet the challenge of the future'.

The professional ethic

It would be inappropriate to continue the discussion further without emphasising the particular mark of a profession concerned with its ethic. 'Adheres to a code of conduct based on ethical principles.' Such established standards of professional conduct are usually referred to as a code of ethics but it must be stressed that this code is based on principles which are a guide to action and not a prescription for action, as the professional nurse has to make personal decisions for nursing activities which, when they are 'safe' and in the interests of the patient or client, are ethical and professional but if they are not safe and not in the interests of the patient or client are unethical and unprofessional. Being a member of the nursing profession therefore entails embracing and internalising a professional ethic.

Most of the professions calling themselves a profession have a code of conduct to guide their members in their dealings with clients and other professionals. Comparing the codes of conduct of different professions, one is struck by the similarities rather than difference between them. Common elements which are characteristic of the professional ethic can therefore be established (Rule, 1978). 'All demand excellence in their craft, or at least its pursuit, and all suggest that a profession must subject its activities to critical analysis . . . and all state, in some form, that a professional requires a special and unusual competence because he is concerned with vital needs.' Miss Rule suggests that the professional ethic is a way of life, although she concedes that there may sometimes be problems as to what is the best way of ensuring and maintaining the well-being of patients and clients. But she is in no doubt that 'professional service, once offered, must be as good as the individual can make it and cannot be refused or removed if one is to act in accordance with the professional ethic'. This view received a resounding endorsement during 1978 (and 1980) and 1979 by the Royal Colleges of Nursing and Midwives respectively whose members voted overwhelmingly to voluntarily give up their legal right to strike.

Although a discussion of ethics is more rightly the prerogative of moral philsophers, it is pertinent to consider the topic here in the sociological context of professional nursing in present-day society.

Moral philosophy (and ethics) must be considered in the context of social history, as moral concepts cannot be understood apart from their history for, as MacIntyre (1966) points out, 'moral concepts change as social life changes' not, he hastens to add '*because* social life changes . . . moral concepts are embodied in and are partially constitutive of forms of social life'.

This view is also supported by Maritain (1959). Apart from the 'self-evident primary principle, *good is to be done and evil to be avoided*', Maritain holds that knowledge of natural moral laws is acquired slowly and that the necessary equipment to know the particular precepts of natural law exists within man. This necessary equipment, he says, consists of the 'essential tendencies and inclinations' in man's nature. In other words, our knowledge of moral laws is progressive in nature. The sense of duty and obligation was always present, but the explicit knowledge of the various norms of natural law grows with time.

He cites some examples to support his contention. At one time, he says, and for many centuries, it was considered quite normal to kill prisoners of war who were considered no different to the soldier in combat. Occasionally slavery was exchanged for death but this was considered a favour. But present-day views of obligations to prisoners of war are very different.

Views about obligations to children have also changed. During the industrial revolution using child labour was considered to be quite legitimate, Maritain points out, but society holds a different view now which is 'surely more conformable to natural law'.

The ethics of caring

During the 20th century there has been a great deal of technological innovation and change brought about by extension of knowledge by increased scientific investigations. Some might want to endow the 20th century with the attribute of being the age of technological and scientific progress. Undoubtedly there has been much technological and scientific change, but change and progress are not always or necessarily synonymous terms.

Technological and scientific innovations in health care, are often perceived as revolutionary; but very quickly yesterday's revolutionary treatments become today's common-or-garden treatments. Treatment on artificial kidney machines and blood transfusions are typical examples.

But the recent changes and innovations fostered by technology and science bring with them greater ethical dilemmas for health care practitioners than in any previous century.

THE DILEMMA OF SCIENCE

Science now enables medical practitioners to do extraordinary things such as transplanting human organs and it also has helped a long way towards describing man in society in fundamental terms. But science does not explain man in terms that are comprehensible to him or to other human beings. It deals with cold, hard, objective facts and takes no account of values. The more science helps towards improving knowledge of man and the universe, the more it intensifies the mysteries about them.

It is difficult to agree on how science can always be best used in the interests of man and society, for the body of knowledge of science is useless if there is no common philosophy of life held by those who wish to use the knowledge for the benefit of man.

This poses particular dilemmas in health care for this often entails dealing with life and death matters and involves making decisions about the value and quality of life.

Moral dilemmas

It is comparatively easy to 'moralise' about what is or is not moral, particularly if certain acts denounced as amoral are compatible with ones own outlook on life. Whilst conceding that it is difficult, Clark-Kennedy (1969) suggests that morality is 'the right way of behaving in certain situations' and argues that what man or government ought to do in certain circumstances must be anchored to three things: to natural law, to the welfare of society, and to the concept of personal integrity.

A natural law, in his view, emanates traditionally from a personal God and relates to right and wrong. The authority for deciding right and wrong is sought in general principles laid down, for example, in the Ten Commandments. 'Right and wrong on this view just exist, like space, time and gravitation, although the laws which govern them are much more difficult to elucidate.' There is also another difficulty in accepting this view of the natural law as it is based entirely on the Judeo-Christian tradition. Rationalists might also argue with some justification that anthropologists' observations on primitive tribes and sociologists' observations on certain subgroups in developed societies suggest that there is nothing very 'natural' about this law at all.

That morality should be anchored to the welfare of society was the philosophy that appealed to the utilitarian philosophers of the nineteenth century, who included J.S. Mill among their numbers. Moral acts in their view were those which made for the greatest happiness of the greatest number. There was no appeal to abstract principles. But what is the greatest happiness? If a government has two propositions either to build a holiday camp for 2000 people or a hospital for 2000 people, can a decision be made on this basis? Or even if the choice is between a holiday camp for 200 people as opposed to a hospital for 2000. It could be argued that holiday camps might provide the greatest happiness for the greatest numbers.

If morality is anchored to the value of personal integrity and if it is believed that a man's duty is to maintain his personal integrity in the interests of society, then this, it could be argued, is also likely to make for the greatest happiness of the greatest number. 'According to this concept, intent is moral if it maintains personal integrity, and thereby furthers the interest of society; amoral, if it impairs his personal integrity, and thereby harms society', Clark-Kennedy contends; a contention that gives rise to the concept of secular, as opposed to religious morality. In practice, he holds, there is little difference between secular morality based on the concept of personal integrity and the natural law based on Judeo-Christian ethics, as the concept of duty to society has the same practical consequences for society as the command to love one's neighbour.

But the interests of self and society often conflict. For example, if a nurse is the only staff member on duty on a particular ward and she suddenly becomes febrile, does she stay on duty knowing that she will not give adequate safe supervision to her patients or does she request sick leave knowing that there will probably be no one to give nursing supervision at all? The funadmental differences in Judeo-Christian and secular ethics is in the nature of the rewards. In the former the reward sought is the greatest happiness of the greatest number in Heaven after death, in the latter the reward sought is the greatest happiness of the greatest number on the earth during life.

The actual dilemmas

The main moral problems in health care today are those concerned with stopping life starting, terminating life when it has started, enabling to live and letting the sick individual die.

STOPPING LIFE STARTING

Contraception is widely available today under the National Health Service. Sessions are held at large numbers of health centres and health clinics at which prescriptions for contraceptive pills and devices are available without difficulty to both men and women, some of whom are very young indeed, some unmarried, some promiscuous.

Should the promiscuous young girl of 14 be put on the pill by a doctor and counselled in its use by a health visitor when there might be risks to the destruction of the personal integrity of the individual at the expense of society? The alternative being an unwanted illegitimate child.

Sterilisation as a form of birth control is also available to both men and women. Is it moral to deprive an individual of the right of parenthood for ever? If a mother has had more children than she can cope with and for a variety of reasons finds that she cannot use conventional birth control methods, it might be argued that sterilisation would maintain her personal integrity and create greater happiness for her family because their care would not in future be diluted by another unwanted child. But if at some future time a desire for more children could not be satisfied because of the operation, could it then be deemed to have been an amoral act?

In India, where demand for food greatly exceeds supply and where the general educational levels are not conducive to using other birth control methods, control of population by using sterilisation methods might be argued to be ethical on the basis of enhancing personal integrity and greatest happiness.

TERMINATING LIFE WHEN IT HAS STARTED

Another, commonly used method of birth control is abortion which involves killing the unborn fetus. The attitudes to this practice vary widely ranging from it being considered murder because it kills a living human being to accepting that the practice is ethical if the abortion is performed in the interests of the woman's health or in the interests of her other children's welfare. This secular moral stand is in fact enhanced in British law.

With advances being made in amniocentesis, the screening of antenatal patients for abnormality will eventually become part of the regular antenatal care given to expectant mothers. It has been argued by Butler (1971) that this would have economical benefits for society as 'it would be significantly less costly to find and abort the trisomy 21 fetus before birth than to maintain the mongol child in a special institution afterwards?' On that basis it might be conceded that amniocentesis was both desirable and ethical but it must be remembered that, as yet, the long-term effects of amniocentesis on fetuses is not known.

British society recognised the dilemmas facing numbers of doctors and nurses when the Abortion Act of 1967 was enacted and attempted to alleviate the difficulties by writing a 'conscience clause' into the Act which enables any doctor, nurse or health care worker to refuse to participate in surgical abortion if they have a conscientious objection to the procedure. But the conscience clause itself, not surprisingly, provokes more problems than it was designed to solve, as Campbell (1975) succinctly indicates:

'Nurses are placed in a considerable dilemma when asked to carry out treatment by medical staff which is contrary to what they believe is right. Should students who have strong moral convictions in this area be asked to train in gynaecological wards where their principles cannot be taken fully into account? In practice it is now very difficult to dissociate yourself completely from termination of pregnancy. Formerly there was a clearer demarcation between directly helping in theatre and being indirectly involved in post-operative care. Now, with the advent of intravenous Pitocin drips the night nurse may be counting the drops and changing the rate without realising that this is the latest way of being directly involved. Some students decide that, since whatever they do, the work will proceed, they ought to take their share of it.'

So even if a nurse finds abortion amoral, her sense of obligation to colleagues might superimpose itself so that she is almost forced into ordering her ethical priorities. Her dilemma is made none the easier by citing Gardner (1972) who points out that 'periodically during abortion debate, letters appeared in the press from deformed adults or children, a group of thalidomide victims among them, stating that they are glad to be alive and grateful that no one had aborted them'.

ENABLING TO LIVE

Great efforts are made to keep every newborn infant alive in spite of the fact that one in every 75 infants is sufficiently abnormal to demand some kind of action or special care.

Because of progress in surgery an increasing number of congenital defects can be rectified, but not all. This means that increasing numbers of handicapped children are surviving. This creates great demands on the families for support and from society to provide resources for their care either in institutions or in the community.

The revolution in health care caused by antibiotics has also extended the life expectancy of the elderly. They grow older and live to die of different diseases.

The young and middle-aged also live longer. Much more can be done for the treatment of chronic diseases. Even those suffering from paralysis and unconsciousness can be kept alive almost indefinitely as a result of a combination of care, technology and antibiotics.

All this has raised the life expectancy for all age groups. But what about the quality of life to the individual and the costs to society? Large numbers of residents occupy institutions for the chronic sick, mentally handicapped, head and spinal injuries, and geriatric hospitals.

There are some who would argue that euthanasia should be legalised to control the situation. But euthanasia, it could be argued, is killing and therefore against the natural law. So, it could be retorted, is abortion but this has been accepted by British law on the basis of secular morality. But suicide or self-killing is, since 1961, no longer a criminal act. Can the law be changed to reflect the change in society's attitudes if supportive attitudes towards euthanasia develop? When that happens the dilemmas already created for some by the Abortion Act might be posed all over again.

No final conclusion

But there is more to the study of ethics than consideration of causing death and prolonging life. Indeed, if nurses develop the political consciousness advocated by Schröck, fundamental ethical issues will inevitably come to demand their attention. Issues concerning social security and the equitable distribution of health resources between different geographical areas and between institutional and non-institutional care budgets.

In these days when some parts of the United Kingdom have more medical specialists than others, when teaching hospitals are allocated greater resources than non-teaching hospitals, when vast amounts of human and financial resources are sought for experimental surgery and when management decisions have to be made about investment in prevention or cure, the ethics of decision-making pose a dilemma that no professional nurse can escape from.

The purpose of this discussion is not to supply answers to dilemmas but to discuss the dilemmas. For what is right in one situation for an individual nurse may be wrong for another nurse in the same situation or for that same nurse in a different situation.

The ethical problems in health care are succinctly assessed in my view by Maclean (1975) when she says:

'There are no easy answers to the issues raised, but in the final analysis we would do well to remember that as human beings we are in no position to act as judges over those whom we profess to serve and care for. However, in nurse education we should not be so busy discussing the advances which lead to the dilemmas, that we have no time to spare for thought as to the dilemmas themselves.'

ETHICS OF NURSING PRACTICE

Of great ethical importance are those day-to-day decisions that the nurse makes as an autonomous professional practitioner. Are these decisions based on established nursing knowledge, myth or tradition? Are nursing activities, such as treating pressure sores, carried out on the basis of research findings, or as a result of culpable ignorance of them? Is a nurse always justified in using her time to 'do' things for a patient awaiting surgery when an informed talk might meet his real needs and enhance his postoperative care? Is a nursing practitioner justified in carrying out nursing procedures for which she has not been adequately prepared? Does the nurse contribute to those negative aspects, such as noise, which have harmful affects on acutely ill hospital patients? Is a nurse justified to jealously guard 'confidential' information from other professional colleagues when it would be in the patient's interest to share it with them? What are the ethical implications of the 'conspiracy of silence' which keeps information from the patient about his disease or prognosis?

If the nurse is a member of a professional body, she is an autonomous practitioner and therefore entirely, and solely responsible and accountable for her professional activities. There can be no higher authority than her own professional ethic.

That the nurse's professional ethic must take precedence over her legal right to strike was made quite explicit in a statement issued in 1979 by the General Nursing Council for England and Wales, the statutory body responsible for basic training, examination and registration of nurses in England and Wales: 'The General Nursing

Council for England and Wales has decided to make a pronouncement on whether a nurse who limits or withdraws his or her services could face proceedings for professional misconduct. The Council is of the opinion that if a nurse puts the health, safety or welfare of his or her patients at risk by taking strike or other industrial action he or she would have a case to answer on the score of professional misconduct, just as he or she would if the health, safety or welfare of patients were put at risk by any other action on his or her part.'

AN INTERNATIONAL CODE FOR NURSES

At the Grand Council meeting of the International Council of Nurses (ICN) held in São Paulo, Brazil, in July 1953 an international code for nurses was adopted for the first time. This was subsequently revised by the Grand Council meeting in Frankfurt, Germany, in June 1965. A new code was later produced by the ICN's Professional Services Committee and adopted at a meeting of the Council of National Representatives of ICN in Mexico City in May 1973.

There can be no once and for all answers in a discussion of the ethics of health care. 'But even if total explanations are no longer possible', Warnock (1960) argues in a commendable pragmatic fashion, 'that is no reason why we should not still look at human beings in general in their context in the world. If we do this, it is likely that the most important thing about them should appear to us to be their capacity for acting spontaneously, and choosing between alternatives; for making and keeping resolutions, for regretting their decisions and rationally changing their minds, for feeling guilt and feeling pride in their achievements . . . it has too often been suggested, without sufficient support, that all decisions must be decisions on *principle,* or decisions to do something *because it is a duty*', but she adds, 'not all moral decisions are of this kind; and indeed that sometimes to do something on the supposition that it is a duty, waiting to be fulfilled, would be bad faith'.

DEVELOPMENT OF THE NURSING PROFESSION IN THE UNITED KINGDOM

Some confidence in the claim for a professional identity for nursing can, in my view, be made but, as in most developments, professional and otherwise, the present position of the nursing profession can be more fruitfully understood in the perspective derived from considering its history. It will, at least, prevent over-confidence or complacency developing.

Some nursing reports

Dr Magda Kelber (1957), in a foreword to an International Council of Nurses publication on basic nursing education, concluded after reviewing the results of an investigation carried out in 26 countries that certain distinct international trends were indicated. Among other things it was noted that:

1. The emphasis had clearly shifted over the years from 'training' to 'education'—'helping students to grow as whole persons while also requiring the maximum professional efficiency'.
2. There had been a gradual transition from the apprenticeship system to the establishment of schools in which students have full student status and 'where their activities are determined by educational considerations only, rather than by the needs of a hospital or a community'.

In the past few decades there has undoubtedly been a keen and growing interest in, and concern about, nursing education in most countries of the world and also in the United Kingdom. This interest and concern has been documented in a number of publications, some of which are referred to below.

Since the report of the *Lancet Commission on Nursing* (1932) was published, wastage of nursing students has been a major preoccupation of many reports. One third was reported to have 'wasted' in 1932, 37 per cent in 1947 according to the *Report of the Working Party on the Recruitment and Training of Nurses* and a similar figure prevails today.

In 1932 causative factors were held to be age of entry, duty hours, working conditions, study demands, social life restrictions, etc. The 1947 report said about nursing students that 'they are expected to work and train under conditions which even many of those suitably equipped are not prepared to tolerate'. According to the mass media those words have a familiar ring today. Interestingly enough, an investigation carried out for the working party who prepared the 1947 report suggested that there were no significant differences between those who 'wasted' and those who completed training.

This conclusion finds some support in MacGuire's review of over 60 studies of nursing student wastage in *Threhold to Nursing* (1969): 'The attempt to demonstrate the relationships of each of these things separately to withdrawal has not been particularly successful.' A more recent study by Birch (1975) suggests that the only difference between 'wasters' and 'stayers' is that the former are more vulnerable. In fact quite a lot of research has been documented about 'wasters' but very little, if any, about the kind of people who persevere with nursing courses, or their subsequent careers and life styles. Perhaps some future research activity will help fill these gaps in knowledge.

Whether nursing students should be apprentices or students has also been a topic of regular debate. The 1932 report suggested that, as an experiment, some hospitals should employ non-salaried probationers, but offer them 6 weeks holiday each year and 2 separate weeks study leave. Scholarships might be offered, it was suggested, 'until the scheme became well known'.

However, in the *Report of the Nursing Reconstruction Committee* (1945) it was recommended that the nursing student should be considered to be a student and the idea of paying salaries to nursing students was frowned upon. After weighing up the advantages and disadvantages of an apprenticeship system, a 'middle' course was chosen, as there is 'nothing incompatible between apprenticeship and studentship' and the position of trainee engineers was cited in support. Twenty-eight weeks of study during training were recommended. Twenty-four years later, the 1969 SRN syllabus of the General Nursing Council for England and Wales finally implemented that particular recommendation.

The 1947 report called for 'complete student status' which was reiterated in the ill-fated report of the Royal College of Nursing, *A Reform of Nursing Education* (1964).

But it was again accepted in the *Report of the Nurse Tutor Working Party* (1970) that nursing training was 'both a studentship and apprenticeship . . . which corresponds in essence' with what is provided for students of other professions. Can nursing students be real students when in reality they make up the bulk of the hospital nursing service? Can they be apprentices when there are very few skilled craftsmen in the form of trained nurses around on the wards? Those are profound philosophical questions.

Although the nurse tutor working party report held that service needs should not disrupt the pattern of nursing education, it somewhat hastily added that it was essential not to 'lose sight of service realities' which could suggest a curious mixture of professional concern and political cunning. However, future developments might indicate that this report sowed some very fertile seeds.

Where should nursing be taught?

Calls for independently financed schools of nursing were made in all three reports cited above. To some extent this has been realised by the creation of regional (formerly area) nurse training committees. The 1945 report held that the first essential in the establishment of true nursing education is the clear separation between the training of nurses and the obligations to provide nursing services. Incidentally, there were nursing students on the nursing reconstruction committee and they felt strongly that such 'separation' was more important than increased salaries.

The suggestion of university schools of nursing was aired as long ago as 1932 and eventually the first advanced basic nursing courses were introduced in 1957 and are now well established in a number of British universities and polytechnics. The extension of these courses led to the formation of the Association of Integrated and Degree Courses in Nursing in 1969 which, since 1973, holds an annual open conference on topics relating to advanced nursing education.

The 1932 report recommended that tutors should be appointed to be fully involved in education and a tutor/student ratio of 1 : 60 was suggested. The 1945 report suggested a ratio of 1 : 50 and the 1970 report a ratio of 1 : 30. In fact, the present recommended ratio is 1 : 15. Regretfully, an investigation conducted by Dufton (1968) among tutors indicated that tutors were rapidly becoming a geriatric group with 37 per cent over the age of 50 and retirements were occurring at the rate of 3.7 per cent (52) per year. This predicted a nurse tutor shortage which has recently become a stark reality.

Perhaps a very pertinent question is: why is it that more able young nurses do not become teachers of nursing? And why have a number of able nurse teachers moved on to other fields of nursing?

It may be hard to believe, but it has to be conceded that there have been some positive developments in nursing education during the past 40 years in the United Kingdom.

Statutory bodies responsible for basic nurse training now insist on a minimum number of weeks for theoretical study and have imposed restrictions on the minimum and maximum number of weeks allocated to clinical units and limited the amount of night duty undertaken by nursing students. And there are tutors and some clinical teachers around (during the day) with the sole responsibility for teaching. In some respects therefore it could be argued that students' educational needs are now being considered to some great extent and are given some priority. A mark of a profession is that it controls its own professional education, it will be recalled.

THE ART AND SCIENCE OF NURSING

Most professions tend to be preoccupied with role; so let us now examine the nurse's role and the art or science of nursing.

The nursing profession is understandably constantly concerned about the nurse's role and the tasks and activities relevant to that role, but there appears to be no concensus about the central idea of nursing, which is necessary to give those tasks and activities their reasons for existence and this poses a dilemma for nursing education and any programme for teaching nursing care.

Some current opinions on nursing developed in greater detail by an American nurse, Professor Gertrude Ujhely (1968), are worthy of consideration. All nurses would without exception agree that the main concern of nursing is the patient. Some might stress the whole patient 'in all his dimensions—physical, emotional, social and spiritual' and a glance at the SRN syllabus of the General Nursing Council for England and Wales will confirm that some attempt has been made to encourage schools of nursing to foster an awareness in nursing students of the total needs of their patients.

In the early part of this century the nurse was mainly seen as the physician's assistant who, by her persuasion, induced the patient to use his will to live and get better. And sometimes it worked. Times have changed, however, and today the focus of nursing inevitably goes far beyond being merely an extension of the physician's role. The hand maiden image has gone—forever.

It could also be suggested that nursing is providing comfort and it is true that that is the nurse's principal function in many cases but often, as is well known, the nurse cannot afford to keep the patient 'comfortable' for that would result in maintaining or aggravating his ill condition, even though attempts to keep discomfort to a minimum should always be maintained.

It could also be suggested that nursing provides an optimal environment for the patient. This idea has been extended in psychiatry and mental-handicap care to include the emotional climate in the unit and concepts such as the 'therapeutic community' and 'home atmosphere' may be familiar to you. But this leads on to the considerations of whether the nurse should be a co-ordinator and/or monitor of care or a practitioner at the bedside. Perhaps to prevent role conflict, which can be very painful, many nurses and others consider that the nurse *cares* for patients. Indeed the Briggs Report calls nursing the major caring profession, it will be recalled.

Care is a good term, for nurses do administer care to the patient and do care what happens to him. But care, defined by the Oxford Dictionary as (occasion for) solicitude, anxiety; serious attention, is not really specific enough.

And what about the idea of caring for the *whole* patient? In other words giving the patient total care by meeting all his needs. Can any one person really meet the total needs of another for any length of time? It is open to reasonable doubt. Some patients, it could be argued, probably do not want total care from nurses in the first place.

All they want and perhaps all they need from nurses might be instruction about how to manage their colostomies or catheters or prostheses and all the paraphernalia that go with caring for such things. It is quite possible that if one tries to find out how they are getting along at work and with their families, these patients might well think such enquiries were imposing on their privacy. They may be proud. They may only want what *they* think they need from nurses, and no more. Nurses and all other health care workers have to accept that the patient's needs as perceived by him have to be met.

It could also be held that nursing is a helping relationship. True again, but isn't it true of a number of other health and social welfare professions? 'Helping' like 'caring' is an attractive term but it, too, is not specific enough.

That nursing is helping patients to learn from their experience is another appealing contention.

But sometimes the patient does not want to learn. Some do not have the mental or physical strength to cope with a deeper understanding of themselves. Many patients do not want or cannot, for a variety of reasons, accept this help of the nurse, particularly many patients who are in intensive care units and in hospitals for the mentally sick and mentally handicapped, for example.

Then there is the often repeated remark: 'Nursing has not yet been defined'. Many argue that it is essential to define *nursing* before deciding on what constitutes nursing practice and therefore what should be taught to nursing students. Professor Jean McFarlane (now Baroness McFarlane of Llandaff), professor of nursing in the Manchester University, made the point forcefully at a King's Fund Centre Conference reported in *Nursing Mirror* (Smith, 1969) when she said that there were a great number of research studies about *nurses* but hardly any about *nursing*. Since then some attempts have been made to fill the gaps in nursing knowledge by studies of nursing care carried out, as already noted, by nurse-researchers at the Royal College of Nursing and in nursing departments in universities and polytechnics, but it will be some time yet before a substantial body of knowledge about nursing is produced. Others, whilst agreeing that nursing needs defining, claim that the definition of nursing is intimately connected with knowledge of man—the more is known about man, the better one shall know what nursing is, or should be, about and Chapman's view, already cited, gives some support to this thesis. That is a very plausible argument, and certainly, a case for inclusion of biological, medical and social sciences into nursing course curricula would hardly be challenged by anyone, but man needs care *now*! He cannot wait for an extension of knowledge and in any case a central focus is necessary around which to organise this knowledge so that it will be meaningful for nurses and professional colleagues.

But what is the central focus of nursing? According to the American Nurses Association the 'essential components of professional nursing are care, cure and co-ordination', a statement that certainly helps synthesise all these different opinions and is not merely another illustration of transatlantic jargon.

The questions 'What is nursing?' and 'What is unique in nursing?' will plague the nursing profession for some time to come. Perhaps that is why so much time is spent discussing and arguing about so-called non-nursing duties: it's easier until an informed conclusion can be made about what comprises the unique body of knowledge that belongs to nursing. Such a body of knowledge is considered essential, if nursing is to claim the right to be called a profession and will only come about with a rapid extension of a scientific and philosophical spirit of enquiry within members of the nursing profession; qualities that are not always particularly well developed during basic nursing courses presently offered—nor in most of the post-basic nursing courses for that matter. But nursing is on the way there.

The real concern of nursing

What then should be the *real* concern of nursing? It is difficult to provide an answer to that question, but one way of getting out of the dilemma, Professor Ujhely suggests, is to accept *sustaining the patient* as the real concern of nursing, whilst conceding that it need not be the only solution. This particular perspective on nursing has a commendable appeal.

Over a hundred years ago Florence Nightingale wrote that nursing 'is to put the patient in the best condition for nature to set upon him'! That idea is still sound enough today and needs only rephrasing in the light of present-day nursing practice. Today's patient needs not only to overcome illness, but often needs help in adjusting to it and help in his rehabilitation. Surgical and medical treatments are continually being improved and new methods innovated, all of which increases the intensity of the patient's care. And as the numbers of elderly in the population increase, the demands for caring rather than curing will be intensified. The patient is therefore 'in desperate need of someone whose expertise consists of *sustaining him in his experience* of struggle, whether it be the crisis of a serious accident or emergency operation, childbirth or the death of a close relative, having to live with one's tendency to project one's shortcomings onto others, relearning to speak after a cerebral accident, or facing death after repeated heart attacks or in the last stages of leukaemia'.

Who can do this better than the nurse who gives a 24-hour service and who is frequently present with the patient when visited by doctors and other professional workers and often interprets the patient for them?

Sustaining the patient in practice

The following examples of a nurse sustaining a patient in his experience illustrate the nurse at work in an independent professional role with a unique function.

1. A nurse who is assisting a doctor during the examination of a patient's pelvis observes the patient's reactions and notes that he is very tense which makes it impossible for the doctor to carry out the

examination effectively as the tenseness makes it difficult to palpate the patient's pelvic organs.

The doctor asks the patient to breathe deeply so that the examination can proceed.

The nurse, in her unique and professional role, does not simply reinforce the doctor's request to the patient by restating that the patient should breathe deeply to assist relaxation. Instead, she focuses on the patient's experience of the examination. The experience of undergoing an uncomfortable procedure. She may therefore say to the patient 'Hold on to my hand' or 'The examination will be less uncomfortable and over sooner if you take several deep breaths now'. The nurse may even breathe deeply a few times to help the patient get started.

2. A psychiatrist whilst giving therapy to a patient diagnosed as alcoholic is touching on what the patient considers to be very sensitive and upsetting material. This causes the patient to become extremely anxious and frantic. He wants to get out of hospital as quickly as possible so that he can get a drink which he believes will make him feel better.

Since the patient is being treated by a doctor the nurse will not attempt to investigate or analyse the patient's problem alone, nor will she glibly say to him: 'If you drink, we cannot help you'. Instead, the nurse will stay or, at least, offer to stay with the patient while he remains anxious. She may say to him: 'Talk about your problem if you want to', which is quite different from exploring the underlying problem. Any outcome of these discussions will be recorded in the nursing notes which will significantly contribute to decisions about the patient's overall therapy.

In order to help relieve the patient's oral craving, the nurse may offer him a cup of tea or a fruit drink and biscuits. Or she may just sit in silent empathy, where the patient can see her, while he paces up and down the ward.

3. A district nurse calls on an old woman who has recently had surgery for a fractured neck of femur. The family doctor has said that the woman should be out of bed and mobilised but the patient thinks otherwise.

Even though the district nurse introduces herself to the patient and says that she has come to help her get up and explains why, the patient becomes angry and fearful and clings to the sides of the bed and refuses to budge. In the circumstances, the district nurse stays with the patient for a while and does nothing and then gives her care in bed so that the patient can develop some confidence in her nurse by getting to know her a little better. Giving competent and skilful nursing care is a most effective way of gaining the patient's confidence. It is not always necessary to say anything.

The nurse then attempts to find out what the patient is afraid of and usually discovers that the patient is afraid of falling again. The nurse therefore gradually encourages the woman to get used to some simple movement, such as sitting on the side of the bed which at the same time enables the nurse to demonstrate that she is able to give adequate and safe support to the patient. Eventually the patient will be amenable to getting out of bed and sitting in a chair, even though it might take a few days to accomplish this. More general mobility follows. As confidence in the nurse grows, the patient has greater confidence in the nurse's suggestions for extended mobility.

It would of course have been helpful if the district nurse had met the patient before discharge from hospital which would have provided her with the opportunity to anticipate the moves and to rehearse the situation mentally with the patient long before the situation became a reality.

The progress made by the nurse is recorded in the nursing notes for the family doctor's information so that his care and guidance to the patient remains compatible with the professional care being given by his professional nursing colleague.

In each of the above hypothetical but nevertheless commonly found situations the primary concern of the nurse is to sustain her patient in the particular experiences he is undergoing at the time.

Their primary concerns in the care given were not, it should be noted, facilitating the doctor's work in the first illustration cited, nor health education in the second illustration, nor carrying out the doctor's orders in the third.

These three examples illustrate the nurse at work as an independent professional, with a unique function, who makes a nursing assessment and prescribes appropriate nursing care.

This perspective on nursing will also affect the practice of nursing, for the nurse, even when busy, will not treat the patient as an object, but as a being with an 'I' even when he is unconscious. Being sensitive to his experience (extending to those close to him) will cause her to cover the patient even if he is unaware that he is exposed, as often happens, for example, in intensive care units.

This sensitivity to the patient's experience will keep her also from discussing matters concerning him in his presence unless he is to be included in the discussion. This awareness will help her insist that interpersonal contact is not automated in the midst of necessary and extending technological efficiency found in present-day hospitals. There is always time enough for anything that one really wants to do—including giving each patient the individual attention he needs.

The nurse will also concern herself with the objective and real world if the patient's experience is important to her. She will attach importance therefore to well cared-for surgical instruments, to nursing procedures executed with skill and gentleness, and to observations meticulously made and recorded. And she cannot help but be concerned with the right diameter and sharpness of needles for injections and an understanding of monitors and be particularly concerned about aseptic technique and prevention of cross infection.

She will concern herself with the smooth running of the clinical unit and with economical use of material resources and time of nursing colleagues and other health care personnel, for good management is implicit in good care.

And she will always bear in mind that intellectual curiosity, good management, loyalty to the institution and colleagues, and mastery of new skills are commendable, important and necessary attributes in a nurse, but the acquisition and practice of these should not detract from the core concern of nursing—the sustaining of the patient in his experience.

The standards of a nurse, trainee and trained alike, are rigorous and professional in any sense of the word. That the public expect such standards is implicit in the fact that they refer to the nursing *profession*.

Lack of precision in definition

The claim of many professions, including nursing, to professional status has resulted from a lack of precision in defining what a 'profession' really is (Chapman, 1977). In reviewing the literature she identified a number of characteristics commonly attributed to professionals. These include knowledge, authority for action, community sanction and development of a subculture.

Nursing, viewed in the light of these characteristics, and in Chapman's analysis, was found wanting. It was further argued that a major problem could be that in the United Kingdom the term 'nurse' includes a wide range of practitioners. Indeed, this is the case in many other countries as well. Chapman concluded that 'no matter how nursing is viewed, it does possess some serious deficiencies at the moment and if full professional status is to be accorded there must be a revision of some aspects of both organisation and education of the many individuals functioning under the title of nurse'.

Chapman's views have been developed further by Margaret Auld (1979) in a reflection on nursing in a changing society. She focuses in particular on the concepts of 'autonomy' and a 'model of professionalism' and warns that if nurses do not delineate their own professional role others will do it for them by default, which would militate against nurses obtaining any autonomy. Auld also stresses that other health care professionals are attempting to define their individual roles more precisely and this includes elements within the province of nursing.

She expresses a fear about the growth of professionalisation, pointing out that this could lead to too strict demarcation, leaving some patients and clients between the lines of professional demarcation. As a result, close patient—nurse contact would be impaired and there would also be a possibility of open conflict between health care professions. Nurses must develop their own professional model, Auld argues, and they themselves must clearly define their role. Nurses must also 'recognise the frequent need to overlap our role as nurses with that of other professions' to secure the best care for patients and clients.

'As a profession it is not enough to think of practice and to think of professionalism. As a profession we must also think of scholarship: scholarship in the sense that our practice must be built on data. It must be built on research . . . conducted by us nurses who have acquired whatever scientific body in any of those sciences we feel applicable to our endeavour. We must pursue lines of excellence in scholarship in the sense of systematising our practice, which we currently do not do. We must know whereof we speak when we wish to innovate, and we must be scholarly in our understanding of the background of those others with whom we work' (Mauksch, 1971).

INTERPLAY OF RIGHTS AND RESPONSIBILITIES

In a World Health Organisation paper on nursing, Dr Dorothy Hall, the WHO's regional nurse for Europe, has claimed that nursing 'as a profession in its own right and a discreet health discipline' is responsible for planning, organising, implementing and evaluating nursing services as a distinct segment of health care, and for educating practitioners to provide these services. The primary responsibility of nursing, she claims, is to provide care directly to the patient, client, family or community. It is concerned with maintaining, promoting and protecting health, treating the sick and providing rehabilitation. It also deals with psychosomatic and psychosocial aspects of life as these affect health, illness and dying.

If these are pertinent functions of the role of a professional nurse, as well as rights derived from being a nurse, then responsibilities are tremendous and far-reaching, particularly as it is the nurses themselves who claim that nursing is a profession 'in its own right'. Society has not given them that mandate, except indirectly insofar as legislation in some countries forbids the use of the title 'nurse' by any person other than a professionally qualified nurse. In some countries role and function of the nurse are defined in the law.

Since the French Revolution, a Bill of Rights has been regarded as an essential preamble to most Constitutions. The preamble to the Charter of the United Nations (1948) reaffirms 'Faith in fundamental human rights', without, however, saying what these human rights are or should be.

In 1948, after long discussions by the human rights commission of the United Nations, assisted by UNESCO, the General Assembly adopted a universal declaration of human rights. The preamble 'A common standard of achievement for all peoples and all nations . . . to promote respect for these rights and freedoms and by progressive measures, national and international, to secure their universal and effective recognition and observance . . .'. It further declares that 'It is a fundamental human right for every person to have a standard of living adequate to the health and wellbeing of himself and his family including food, clothing, housing and medical care and necessary social services'. These statements of principle are deliberately kept general and, as Benn and Peters (1959) point out, therefore received assent from governments and individuals who often differ radically in their particular judgements and decisions.

Right to health

Nursing care *per se*, is not identified as a right by the United Nations but perhaps nurses can justify their role by consoling themselves with the fact that at its founding the World Health Organisation stated that the 'enjoyment of the highest standard of health is one of the fundamental rights of every human being'. But, of course, it should be stressed that the emphasis is on 'health' and not on sick care.

Many governments have endorsed the citizens' right to health. But the perceptions of this right vary. For example, it was pointed out by Adams (1974) that the Australian's right to health had been endorsed by the Australian government, believing that 'major changes are promised for Australia's health service . . . the reasons for these changes are complex and relate to . . . the advent of a Labour (Social Democratic) Government which views health care as a fundamental right of all citizens'. However, some two years later a fellow Australian doctor saw these changes in a different light: 'Welfare in the best sense of the word is one of the most desirable attributes of a modern state' (Meyers, 1976). But he hastens to ask: 'When will our leaders learn that welfare costs money and that money comes from production? When will our medical policy planners wake up to the probability that the "day nursery" mentality, by encouraging the citizen to look to the state as a crutch and to avoid accepting a measure of responsibility for himself, may ultimately affect the future not only of welfare but of the state itself?'

These two arguments illustrate that what one man perceives as a right another man can perceive as a manifestation of irresponsibility.

Let us now return to the argument of Benn and Peters. They point out that words like 'rights', 'duties', 'ought' and 'obligation' belong primarily to normative discourse. That is, these words are used in prescribing conduct according to rules and have a prescriptive force only if we assume the rule to be enforced, i.e. widely observable. Rules prescribe behaviour, and in so doing are said to impose duties or obligations.

When it is claimed that a nurse has a duty to prevent cross-infection in hospitals, what is really being claimed is that there is a rule that leaves her no choice in the matter. It is required of her as part of the professional responsibility of a nurse. This is not the case with a right. If individuals have a right to health, they may possess health or be persuaded to maintain or neglect health, just as they prefer. Benn and Peters ask in what sense rights can derive from rules, if rules prescribe or require conduct of a particular type? The answer lies in the correlation of rights and duties, such that the right of X is the duty of Y, with the implication that Y has a responsibility to ensure the fulfilment of X's right. To say that an individual has a right to health is to imply that there is a rule which, when applied to the case of the individual and a nurse or other health worker, imposes on the nurse a duty or responsibility to maintain and promote the health of the individual, if the individual so chooses.

'Without the possibility of the correlative duty resting somewhere', the attribution of the right to an individual 'would be meaningless' (Benn and Peters, 1959). At most therefore, a right may entail the act or performance on the part of someone else, and, at least, non-interference on the part of other men generally.

Right and duty

Right and duty are different names for the same normative relation, depending on the point of view from which it is regarded. In other words, the statement of a right is only another form of the statement of a duty. The concepts of duty and responsibility are concepts of modern society (MacIntyre, 1966). In Greek society, there was a preoccupation with concepts such as goodness, virtue and prudence. The respective roles of these concepts hinge upon a central difference between Greek ethics and modern ethics. In general, Greek ethics asks: 'What am I to do if I am to fare well?' Modern ethics asks: 'What ought I to do if I am to do right?' And 'it asks this question in such a way that doing right is made something quite independent of faring well' (MacIntyre 1966). Indeed, as MacIntyre further argues, morality 'cannot have any justification external to itself; if we do not do what is right for its own sake, and whether it is to our interest or not, then we are not doing what is right'.

It is therefore particularly important to bear this in mind when focussing on nurses' rights. For it is true to say that the rights of nurses as citizens of society are those of all other individuals in society, a point pertinently made by Patten, an Australian nurse, at the 16th quadrennial congress of the ICN in Tokyo. In moving to further the rights of nurses, she argued that 'we have a right as nurses to examine some of the issues underlying our planning and action, whether that planning or action is directed specifically towards improving pay, education or the social and cultural conditions in which nursing personnel work'.

No absolution from duty

However, it does not follow that if one individual or society at large fails to respect the rights of nurses, for example in matters related to pay and education, nurses are absolved from their duties and responsibilities to the individual and society. It does not follow that the right to health of members of society is conditional upon their fulfilment of what, in the view of nurses, might be considered society's duty, for example to ensure that nurses have adequate resources for fair pay and good nursing education. As Patten says: 'In essence . . . the nurse . . . can meet his or her obligations appropriately when that person is acting in his or her own right on the basis of his or her own values, beliefs and knowledge, and not simply responding to his or her expectation of others.'

It is also essential, when considering the rights of individuals to health, to bear in mind the warning voiced by Redman (1968). The wellbeing of an individual, she points out, may be poorly served by altering health beliefs so that they do not conform to the cultural norm or so that a denial which is helping to maintain an individual's stability is destroyed. Even if one is convinced that a health belief ought to be changed, reaching this goal can be very difficult because of the complexity of little-understood factors which contribute to a health belief or health action. A factor affecting the possibility of change is that health competes with other values in life for attention which may be more potent or salient for some individuals, for example social approval or freedom from financial worries.

Nurses' responsibilities

Nurses have both individual and corporate responsibilities (Baly, 1975). The prime responsibility of nurses is to protect and enhance the wellbeing and dignity of each individual patient in their care, irrespective of race, colour, creed, or socioeconomic status.

Each individual nurse as an autonomous professional has the same responsibility to be a safe practitioner and has exclusive responsibility for the management of nursing care. There is no point, and indeed in my view it detracts from the nurse's standing as an independant professional practitioner, to expect the organisation to take responsibility for her unsafe practices. Nurses therefore have a responsibility to keep up to date in techniques, knowledge and information which is necessary to ensure the 'safe practice in carrying out the normal standard functions of the job' (Baly 1975).

Nurses have a personal responsibility for effective communications—to the right person at the right time. This includes a special responsibility for ensuring that appropriate and correct information is given to the patient and his relatives during his stay in hospital and before discharge home again. Promotion of health in the community also entails giving accurate and up-to-date health education information. Patients everywhere have the right to know what is wrong with them and they have the right to know their prognoses. Nurses everywhere have therefore individual responsibilities to see that patients get this information. Nurses should never be party to any conspiracy of silence. Nurses also have a responsibility to share information with other professional colleagues. It is a particularly professional activity to decide when to share 'confidential' information with other colleagues. It is, in my view, totally irresponsible to risk mental and physical harm to patients or clients by being possessive of any information, whatever its source.

Accurate record keeping is another important professional responsibility for nurses.

As Baly (1975) indicates, many patients will have a 'multiplicity of health problems some of which will be inter-related with social and economic problems . . . it is of paramount importance that health service workers understand the structure of the health service' and related social, welfare and voluntary services. It is a myth, she argues, that 'with all the services of the mass media people know their rights. Nearly all research into hidden poverty and undisclosed sickness shows that many people, particularly the old, do not know the services to which they are entitled and are often too frightened or too proud to ask'.

Corporate responsibilities, identified by Baly (1975), include responsibility for education and extension of the body of knowledge. For 'to rely on folklore and tradition not only denies clients a more intelligent service, it also makes life dull'. To ensure that this corporate responsibility can be met, Baly holds that nurses need to be organised into a professional organisation committed to fostering the science and art of nursing. This is also a means of formalising and establishing the national power base of the nursing profession.

Political consciousness

Schröck (1977) has stressed that whether nurses like it or not 'the availability and distribution of health care facilities involves political thought and decisions. Those in need, such as the poor or the sick, are usually not part of a very powerful group in society. They are, on the whole, recipients of what others decide is due to them'. I would therefore argue that it is a corporate responsibility of the professional nursing organisation to ensure that the rights of the poor and those in need, in particular, are safeguarded.

Nurses everywhere, if they are to effectively activate their corporate professional responsibility, must foster and nurture political consciousness among members of the nursing profession.

Problems of professionalisation

The problem associated with the professionalisation of nursing is that the setting of goals (i.e. the search for a research base and body of nursing knowledge, establishing education programmes, devising special territorial boundaries, establishing professional organisations and emphasising the personal autonomy of individual nursing practitioners), although highly desirable if seen as a means towards enhancing nursing care delivery and promoting health, may—to the cynical observer—give the impression of coming dangerously close to being an end in istelf. Nurses have an individual and corporate responsibility to ensure that this does not happen.

'As citizens of the state and as private individuals nurses should defend and actively pursue those moral values to which their profession is committed, namely, individual autonomy, parity of treatment and the pursuit of health. In some circumstances this may require protest against, and opposition to, social and political conditions which are detrimental to human wellbeing; and in others, the altering of personal habits which set a poor example in health care. In all other respects nurses have the right to regulate their private lives according to their own standards of morality, provided that their style of life does not cast doubts on the integrity and trustworthiness of their profession' (Royal College of Nursing 1976).

A theoretical approach

Referring to the rights and responsibilities of nurses and patients, Chapman (1980) recommends the social exchange theory as a possible approach to help nurses to conceptualise about rights and responsibilities. She points out that most of the early theorising about social exchange was done by social anthropologists 'who found that while some aspects of social exchange have a complex economic connotation, other aspects appear to be more important for their symbolic value and the social ties they create'. For example, how many nurses, she asks, would assert that the patient has a responsibility to allow nurses to care for them? In such a situation, the patient's dependence is satisfying one of the nurse's psychological needs. 'The nurse may also feel that the patient has a duty to cooperate and be grateful for his care.'

Social exchange theory, Chapman argues, can at least provide a fascinating analysis of the interplay of rights and responsibilities of both nurses and patients.

REFERENCES

Adams, A.I. (1974) Developments in Australia's health services. *International Journal of Epidemiology,* **2** (1) 5–7.

Auld, M.G. (1979) Nursing in a changing society. *Journal of Advanced Nursing,* **4,** 287–298.

Baly, M.E. (1975) *Professional Responsibility in the Community Health Services.* Aylesbury: H M & M.

Benn, S.I. & Peters, R.S. (1959) *Social Principles and the Democratic State.* London: Allan & Unwin.

Birch, J. (1975) *To Nurse or Not to Nurse.* London: Royal College of Nursing.

Butler, L.J. (1971) Human chromosome abnormalities. *Midwife and Health Visitor,* March.

Campbell, A.V. (1975) *Moral Dilemmas in Medicine,* 2nd edn. Edinburgh: Churchill Livingstone.

Carr-Saunders, A.M. & Wilson, P.A. (1964) *The Professions.* London: Cass.

Chapman, C.M. (1974) Nursing education—curriculum content. *Queen's Nursing Journal,* October.

Chapman, C.M. (1977) Concepts of professionalism. *Journal of Advanced Nursing,* **2,** 51–55.

Chapman, C.M. (1980) The rights and responsibilities of nurses and patients. *Journal of Advanced Nursing,* **5,** 127–134.

Clark-Kennedy, A.E. (1969) Moral problems in medical practice. *Nursing Times,* occasional paper, 18 September.

Dufton, A. (1968) *Factors Affecting Recruitment of Nurse Tutors.* London: Kings Fund.

Follett, M.P. (1965) *Dynamic Administration.* London: Pitman.

Gardner, R.F.R. (1972) *Abortion—the Personal Dilemma.* London: Paternoster Press.

Hall, C.M. (1973) *Who controls the nursing profession?* (paper read at the ICN 15th quadrennial congress in Mexico City, May 1973).

Hall, D.C. (1977) A position paper on nursing. *Journal of Advanced Nursing,* **2,** 327–328.

Hall, D.C. (1980) The nature of nursing and the education of the nurse. *Journal of Advanced Nursing,* **5,** 149–159.

International Council of Nurses (1973) *Code for Nurses: Ethical Concepts Applied to Nursing*. Geneva: ICN.
Kelly, C.W. (1968) *Dimensions of Professional Nursing*. New York: Macmillan.
MacGuire, J. (1969) *Threshold to Nursing*. London: Bell.
MacIntyre, A. (1966) *A Short History of Ethics*. New York: Macmillan.
MacLean, D. (1975) Genetics. *Nursing Mirror*, 27 March.
Maritain, J. (1959) *On the Philosophy of History*. London: Bles.
Mauksch, I. (1971) *The Social Significance of Nursing as an Independent Practice*. (paper read at the 25th anniversary conference of the Boston University School of Nursing).
Meyers, D. (1976) Day nurseries and welfare states. *British Medical Journal*, 1, **6024,** 1523–1524.
Nightingale, F. (1860) *Notes on Nursing*. London: Harrison.
Patten, M.E. (1978) The right of nurses. *Journal of Advanced Nursing*, **3,** 419–426.
Royal College of Nursing (1976) *RCN Code of Professional Conduct—A Discussion Document*. London: RCN.
Rule, J. (1978) The professional ethic in nursing. *Journal of Advanced Nursing*, **3,** 3–8.
Schröck, R. (1977) On political consciousness in nurses. *Journal of Advanced Nursing*, **2,** 41–50.
Scott Wright, M. (1974) Nursing—present perspectives and future prospects. *Nursing Mirror*, 31 October.
Smith, J.P. (1969) Implementing nursing research findings. *Nursing Mirror*, 31 March.
Smith, J.P. (1974) Nursing in North America. *Nursing Mirror*, 28 November.
Ujhely, G.B. (1968) *Determinants of the Nurse—Patient Relationship* New York: Springer.
United Nations (1948) *United Nations—General Assembly: Universal Declaration of Human Rights*. New York: United Nations Office of Public Information.
Warnock, M. (1960) *Ethics Since 1900*. Oxford University Press.
Report of the Lancet Commission on Nursing (Lancet Ltd, 1932)
Report of the Nursing Reconstruction Committee (Royal College of Nursing, 1945)
Report of the Working party on the Recruitment and Training of Nurses (HMSO, 1947)
Basic Nursing Education—Principles and Practice of Nursing Education (International Council of Nurses, 1957)
A Reform of Nursing Education (Royal College of Nursing, 1964)
Report of the Committee on Senior Nursing Staff Structure (HMSO, 1966)
Report of the Nurse Tutor Working Party (DHSS, 1970)
Report of the Committee on Nursing (HMSO 1972)
Report of the Royal College of Nursing Working Party on the Clinical Nurse Consultant (Royal College of Nursing 1974)
Briggs Committee on Nursing—the Government's Proposals (DHSS 1974)
Journal of Advanced Nursing (Blackwell Scientific Publication, bimonthly from January 1976)

Hierarchal hospital organisation
What is an organisation?
Social organisations
Present theory
An international survey of health care organisations
The process of change
An executive role for nurses
Trade unions

7

Organisations

'Organisation' implies a group of people working in some structured way towards common ends—the objectives of the organisation. The activities of a particular member of the organisation are structured so as to contribute to its objectives; he has an 'organisational role'. That is not to say that each member of the organisation is, could be, or ought to be completely in agreement with the objects of the organisation, only that there must be some area of agreement. Each individual will bring his own interests, values and criteria to the organisation.

The other basic concept of organisation is the individual role: 'people, to the extent that they are organised, carry specific and differentiated roles' (Rowbottom *et al.*, 1973). The roles in the organisation are given titles so that they can be distinguished from the individuals who fill them from time to time. In hospitals, the titles ward sister, nursing officer, administrator, treasurer, and porter have connotations apart from the personal characteristics of particular ward sisters, nursing officers, administrators, treasurers, and porters. 'The minimum function of a title is simply to distinguish one post from another—theoretically a designating number would do' (Rowbottom *et al.*, 1973).

In fact, in the Salmon Report on senior nursing staff structure in the National Health Service, published in 1966, nursing roles were designated by numbers as well as titles e.g. Chief Nursing Officer

(10), Principal Nursing Officer (9), Senior Nursing Officer (8), Nursing Officer (7), and so on.

The first specification of any role in an organisation is a statement of the duties and functions of the role holder. These are generally given in greater detail in job descriptions. Although the range of authority of the role holder is implied in a role specification it is not always made explicit. For example, it may not always be quite clear whether or not the senior nursing officer has the authority to close the hospital to emergency admissions.

To say that two particular members of the organisation are senior nursing officers is not very clear, as senior nursing officer is a fairly non-specific title. But when the functions of these posts of senior nursing officer are known, i.e. that one senior nursing officer is responsible for the management of the operating theatre nursing services and the other senior nursing officer responsible for nursing personnel services, then that information helps one to focus more specifically on the roles.

An individual role holder in the hospital (or other organisation) is specifically responsible for the way he plays his particular role. The term accountability has been given to this responsibility of the individual role holder to perform his duties as expected by the organisation. 'It implies,' Rowbottom *et al.* suggest, 'the presence of a judge somewhere in the situation . . . armed with "hard" institutionalised sanctions—the right to affect such things as pay, promotion, continued employment or professional membership—as apposed to "softer" sanctions of generalised approval or reprobation possessed by all with whom the performer works.'

Therefore, the hospital as an organisation can be perceived as a group of individuals working in interrelated roles, i.e. roles of porter plus nurse plus doctor plus administrator plus social worker plus therapist, etc. (plus patient). Each role includes the following aspects:

1. The duties or functions of the role holder and the tasks derived from these functions
2. The authority, i.e. the right to act on his own initiative, of the role holder
3. The accountability of the role holder for his performance.

The roles when added together make up the total role structure which is efficient only in so far as the agreed objectives of the organisation are economically achieved.

HIERARCHAL HOSPITAL ORGANISATION

All hospital personnel, with the exception of medical consultants, are organised on the basis of a hierarchy. A hierarchy is a succession of superior/subordinate relationships (Figure 7.1). One characteristic of a managerial hierarchy is that each subordinate has

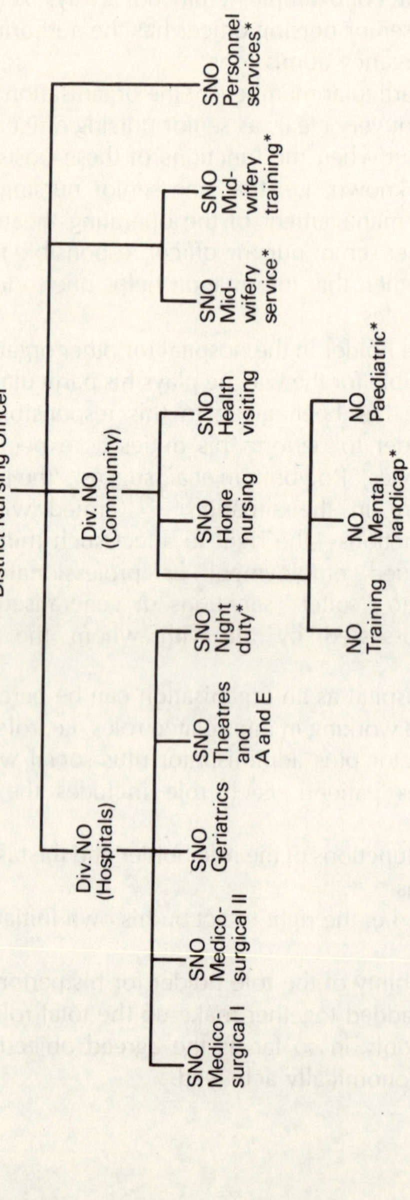

Figure 7.1 Integrated nursing service organisation of the Brent Health District after reorganisation of the NHS in 1974
* Functionally (hospital and community) integrated nursing service.

a clear opportunity to affect policy formation through interaction with his superior. At least he has the opportunity in theory, but in a hierarchy with many layers there is always the inherent danger that communications upwards and/or downwards can be blocked, particularly if one of the intervening managerial roles is filled by an inadequate or pathologically powerful individual.

In a hierarchal organisation it is appropriate that the senior person in the part of the hierarchy concerned should speak for and on behalf of his subordinates. As Rowbottom *et al.* put it: 'One may expect any manager to be able to take an appropriately broad view . . . and it is quite in keeping that he or she should have authority to commit their own staff to action.' If the view, however, is not a broad one serious implications will result for the decision-making process. The senior manager in many hospital hierarchies may require the support of a selected group of immediate subordinates in any discussion or decision-making process. Rowbottom *et al.* point out that this is not the case with consultant medical staff as a whole (or with general practitioners), as their internal relationships are non-hierarchal. But because of the sheer numbers of medical consultants their voice can only be heard through elected representatives.

In the British hospital services, for example, consultant medical staff tend to organise themselves into specialised divisions such as surgical division, medical division, neuro-surgical division, and so on, each electing a chairman who not only conducts the meeting of that division but also represents its members at the district hospital committee (or Medical Executive Committee). In the case of nursing or administration the head of the hierarchy, that is the director of nursing or the director of administration respectively, will speak for all members of their respective hierarchies. But 'the difference between the manager and the elected representative is crucial, since the elected representative . . . will not necessarily be in a position to commit his colleagues or to make decisions which are binding to them' (Rowbottom *et al.*).

Paramedical staff

In the past in the British hospital services, certain classes of paramedical staff such as laboratory technicians, radiographers, physiotherapists and occupational therapists were organised in hierarchies headed by medical consultants. But increasingly mem-

energy to non-productive activity. The point about the inappropriateness of referring to 'the' organisation has already been made and is made even more succinctly by Sackur (1974) who states that: 'Organisations are like hypotheses: they can never be verified, but they are perpetually capable of being falsified. Critical diagnosis of an organisation should be seen as discovering what can be falsified and if necessary changing it. At no time is there any expectation of a perfect solution; only of a more relevant hypothesis.'

There are, however, still severe limitations to the ability to generalise about how health care and hospital organisations work because of the paucity of empirical studies, particularly in the United Kingdom. There is an even greater paucity of cross-cultural studies. In any case, the value of such studies might be doubtful in view of the widely differing health care systems in different countries. Systematic attention has been given to groups of health care workers such as nurses, medical students and administrators but there is a particular lack of knowledge about health care agencies as organisations.

This may be due to the methodological difficulties inherent in trying to maintain normality in health care situations during the period of investigation or to general theoretical inadequacies in the area of study of organisations.

But also because pressures for the efficient use of resources, normally found in industry, might be foreign to British health care workers, as they stand a great distance from the conventional market tests for efficiency and economical use of resources and manpower.

Whilst organisations furnish a common interest for sociologists, they are not necessarily all interested in finding answers to the same sort of questions at all. Work on organisations is found at three levels, depending on what is defined as the dependent variable. The three levels are the behaviour of individual organisation members, the functioning of particular aspects of the organisation and, the level of actions of the organisation involved as a total entity.

SOCIAL ORGANISATIONS

The growth of complex organisations appears to be a critical determinant in the future of society and this has engendered a great deal of concern and interest among economists, political scientists, psychologists and sociologists.

These interests derive from two schools of thought: one developed during the first half of the twentieth century in the action-oriented industrial workplaces, the other derived from the academic interests of some of the founding fathers of sociology such as Max Weber (1946).

In Weber's theory, bureaucracy plays a central role which in his view is the product of a search for rational efficiency. He was therefore interested in the rational means employed to direct the activities of individuals doing various jobs in the organisation towards given objectives.

Weber's model of bureaucracy places emphasis on an 'esprit de corps', a clear-cut division of labour by a system of official duties, the principles of hierarchy, a system of rules, promotions according to seniority or achievement, or both. Activity governed by rules and documents and a system of graded levels of authority based on the strict compliance of subordinates to superiors' commands.

This model was useful for comparing historical and cross-cultural trends but is not very useful for analysing present-day organisations. Weber's model is a functional model and attempts to explain the social structure of the organisation by showing how each of its elements contributes to the persistent and effective operation of the organisation.

But Weber's approach does not reveal the inconsistencies and conflicting tendencies in organisations.

The 'esprit de corps' is unlikely to develop if the characteristic attitude of the members of the organisation is one of reserved detachment. Effective management will then be impeded by the strict exercise of authority in the interests of maintaining discipline, inducing subordinates to conceal operational defects, as they will be anxious to be highly thought of by superiors. This will block the flow of information and will inevitably lead to inefficiency.

Insistence on conformity can make officials' conduct rigid and inhibit rational judgements which are necessary for the efficient performance of tasks. Keeping the rules will not enhance the innovation of new ideas—or necessary change.

If promotion is always based on merit, many workers will never advance in their careers but promotion based on seniority ensures that employees have experience and will foster identification with the organisation. However, promotion by seniority alone does not always foster strong incentives to exert effort and excellence in the job. Indeed the same factors may have both functional and dysfunctional aspects (Merton, 1975), and organisations can be in varying states, at various times, of cohesion, conflict and consensus dependent on the interpersonal relationships between managers and workers.

Furthermore, as Robert Michels (1965) points out, a particular danger inherent in bureaucracy is the *iron law of oligarchy*. He contends that a great deal of energy is directed towards the setting up of the bureaucracy in an effort to produce an efficient organisation. But once the bureaucracy is established the energies are directed at maintaining the bureaucracy. In other words the bureaucracy becomes an end in itself rather than a means towards an end (goal displacement). Reasons for this include the vested interests of officials in maintaining their jobs. Michels' thesis was derived from a critical analysis of the growth of the socialist party.

Other theoretical developments

The work of Weber and his contempories triggered off much debate and as further theoretical developments took place the growth of industrial management interests extended. These were formed and developed in three phases: scientific management, human relations and the personality and organisation approach.

Studies on scientific industrial management conducted by Taylor (1947) emphasised the techniques of controlling workers impersonally by bosses. This approach fostered many time-and-motion studies but it totally disregarded the values and interests of the workers and emphasised impersonal control by supervisors. The period of scientific industrial management is often referred to as the era of organisations without people.

Contrasting dramatically with this impersonal approach is the human relations approach which dominated the 1920s and 1930s. Central to this approach are the personal elements of groups of workers such as morale, job satisfaction and friendship patterns. The manager role is not considered to be one of ensuring compliance of workers but rather of ensuring their cooperation, and emphasis is placed on control and decision making at all levels of the organisation.

The Hawthorne experiments

The human relations approach encouraged students of organisations to investigate the motives of the acceptance of authority by subordinates. The most famous and classic study was conducted in the 1930s at the Western Electric Hawthorne Works in Chicago by a group of social scientists from Harvard University who, as well as adding to the body of knowledge of social science, hoped to improve output and satisfaction at the Hawthorne Works.

A controlled experiment was conducted in an attempt to determine the effect of lighting, length of worker's day, rest pauses, changes in hours of work and so on upon productivity. It was demonstrated that any change in the physical environment produced favourable results but productivity often reached a high level when the original conditions were returned to. Even when the working day was lengthened and the rest pauses reduced, there was no detectable depressing effects on productivity. What the experiment did indicate, however, was that productivity was affected less by working conditions than by the personal involvement of the workers in the experiment. Because they felt they had been singled out to join in the experiment, they were taking more pride in their jobs. (Researchers now often refer to the 'Hawthorne effect' in their own work.)

The investigators changed their methods and from then on emphasis was placed on studying the informal organisation and attitudes on social relationships to work and supervisory behaviour.

It was concluded that attention should be directed to defining the supervisor's role and his selection and training because, it was argued, his behaviour was a major influence on morale. Perhaps there would be less tension in present-day nursing service organisations if this long-established finding was applied to the role and functions of the nursing officer.

Another recommendation made by the investigators was that workers should be given an opportunity for confidential interviews so that they could complain, suggest or express their feelings freely. There is, in theory at least, an opportunity for this during the annual appraisal interviews afforded to all trained nurses in the National Health Service but unfortunately no investigator has attempted to assess their effects on health care productivity!

PRESENT THEORY

A logical outgrowth of the scientific management school of thought is the formal decision-making theory. This theory delineates the logically available alternatives for solving a particular problem and fixes the probability of their outcome. The underlying assumptions are that the workers will seek to reduce risks of failure and to maximise their gains, that they will have the rational capacity to determine the outcomes of alternatives, and that they will have a choice.

A fifteen-year study on management procedures reported by Likert (1967) updated the human relations approach. In a comparison of low-producing and high-producing managers he found that the latter had the tendency to be more interested in the personal problems of employees and less interested in the logical distribution of jobs and tasks. They also tended to exert less pressure on personnel to produce, to supervise subordinates less closely and to be more understanding of poor work performance.

Both of these schools—formal decision-making theory and the human relations approach—have usually satisfied the same objective, viz. to improve the productivity and efficiency of organisations. The understanding of the structure and functioning of the organisation has seldom been the primary objective.

In his study of hospitals, Argyris (1954) emphasises the conflict between personality and organisation and concludes that the general preference in organisations for dependent, placid and submissive employees suppresses the personality needs for challenge, independence and variety of mature individuals. While this approach treats the organisation as a setting for studying personality problems and even though it illuminates the nature of the organisation it is not the primary focus of analysis.

AN INTERNATIONAL SURVEY OF HEALTH CARE ORGANISATIONS

A survey of health care organisation conducted in twenty countries by Maxwell (1974) indicates that governments have tended to assume a gradually increasing role in health care provision.

'The evolution of health systems has been rather like the development of railways. Initially health services, like railroads, sprang up unevenly through local initiative in response to local needs. Before long they found themselves obliged by increasing overlaps and interdependencies to combine and rationalise their operations, though their response was often slow and reluctant.'

Although this trend appears to be an international phenomenon, no two countries have been affected by it in the same way and using the two parameters of where the money comes from, and who runs the health care system—a spectrum is suggested ranging between the extremes of the systems in the USA and the USSR.

In the USA, the health care system is still a free enterprise system of which nearly two thirds is financed by individuals or private voluntary insurance schemes, and marked by inadequate service in some areas and extensive overlap in other areas. Whereas in the USSR the health care system is entirely financed by the central government and controlled administratively by a hierarchy of medically qualified administrators. Services are planned and operated by districts where the 'polyclinic' (Smith, 1963) is a common feature of the health care system.

Other countries' health care systems fall somewhere between the two extremes.

Changes in health care systems are often made against strong and bitter oppositions. Common topics for debate are the appropriate mix of public and private financial contribution to health care, the type of control on expenditure, the need for centralisation or decentralisation and so on.

Even countries as similar and geographically close as the Scandinavian countries can have fundamentally different health care systems for mothers and children (Smith, 1967) and for the mentally handicapped (Smith, 1968), which supports Maxwell's view that 'the mixture of private and public finance considered to be appropriate for a given country and the extent of centralisation or decentralisation of control is influenced by basic convictions about the rights and duties of individuals and the proper role of the state'. Ideological and historical influences on the innovation, development and maintenance of health care organisations cannot be underestimated. But there are advantages and disadvantages in the health care systems at each point in the spectrum, and Maxwell holds that:

'At the United States end, the best medical care may equal or surpass the best available elsewhere, and medical progress is at its most rapid, but at the same time there is gross neglect of some real needs. At the other extreme the peaks and valleys of health care are levelled out; standards are more uniform and there is greater equity, but something is sacrificed by way of excellence and speed of development. Too tightly centralised administration, moreover, carries with it serious risks of rigidity, inefficiency and inability to respond to local needs and conditions.' But he concedes the difficulty in finding ways of controlling finances properly with decentralised administration, and in finding ways of permitting local involvement within the necessary constraints of a national system.

'Policy makers in different countries will inevitably develop different solutions . . . what is important is that they consciously approach the organisation of their health services as a means to an end . . . rather than allow it to become a battleground for interest groups, a focus of ideological conflict, or an end in itself.'

No simple pattern of health care organisation appears to be universally applicable; certain problems appear to be more or less persistent in health care organisations which, Maxwell argues, should serve as a checklist for policymakers that will help them in assessing their own country's health services. The problems are 'barriers to patient access', 'failure to assign or act on essential responsibilities' and 'excessive complexity or cost'.

Barriers to access of health care

The health care organisation can at its best facilitate patient access but at its worst create barriers to the patient. The simplest barrier is non-availability because resources are lacking or because it is impossible to use available resources because of, for example, transport and communication difficulties. In a private fee-paying health care system, lack of personal wealth is also a barrier to obtaining care.

'A final barrier, of growing importance, is the ever-increasing complexity of delivery systems that makes it difficult for people to find their way through the maze, to an appropriate source of help . . .'

Inflexibility of resource use

In large organisations such as health care organisations management of resources tends to be compartmentalised and this can impede the movement of resources from one part of the organisation to another. Until 1975 British National Health Service administrators were found to be inflexible with the financial allocations for capital and revenue expenditures—and moreover had to spend the budgets in any one financial year or lose the monies! However the issue of certain official recommendations in a letter from the Department of Health and Social Security on 9th July on *Flexibility in the use of financial resources* heralded an end to this inflexibility.

Similar problems of inflexibility can be encountered when there are organisational boundaries between preventive and curative services, hospital and community services, and health and social services. To some extent these have been overcome in the United Kingdom since the introduction of the reorganised Health Service in April 1974 but, with the exception of Northern Ireland, there is still a dysfunctional organisational boundary between health and social services in the districts as these two services are managed by different authorities.

The use of resources can also be hampered by professional demarcations. It is very rare, for example, for general practitioners to be able to provide and supervise treatment of their patients in hospital. The patient must normally first be referred to a medical hospital-based consultant.

Merely eliminating barriers, however, is not enough without some vigorous re-allocation of resources which does not as yet appear to have happened in Britain where 'the same regions are relatively rich and poor in hospital provision as a quarter of a century ago,' due in Maxwell's view, to inertia rather than avarice. However some attempt is being made to rectify this by a RAWP formula.

'No country, it seems . . . has yet devised a fully satisfactory mechanism for flexible deployment, coordination and management of all its health care resources.'

Ill defined responsibilities

These problems can range from no one taking responsibility for making a decision to decision being taken under the serious handicap of poor or no information on the adequacy of existing services, health care needs, manpower availability and need, or the cost benefits to the nation of investment in health care. Health care development in the United Kingdom—and in most other countries for that matter—has been very piecemeal in the past but the Government hopes to remedy this by fostering a more vigorous approach to short-term and long-term planning. In the Department of Health and Social Security's draft *Guide to Planning in the National Health Service* (1975) the introduction states:

'Planning is not a new activity in the Health Service. What is new, is the opportunity afforded by reorganisation for health care planning to be comprehensive—.'

'Whilst planning needs to be flexible . . . it must also be directed towards recovering the existing substantial inequalities of care and provision between regions, areas and districts—.'

'Any planning system must essentially be of an evolutionary nature—.'

'There can be no doubt that a balanced planning system will prove to be of immense importance to the National Health Service of the future—.'

It is ironical that the document should appear some 27 years after the first introduction of a British National Health Service organisation. Nevertheless, by 1981, the planning system was more organised.

Needless complexity and cost

Administrative costs, Maxwell states, tend to be low, but unfortunately administration tends to be ineffective as often too much of the money spent on administration tends to go on complex procedures for collection and distribution of funds. He further notes that the movement to rationalise health care systems on a national scale tends to create unnecessarily large and complicated superstructures.

Four principal lines of action are necessary in Maxwell's view if administrators are to make clear decisions unhampered by structural forces in the organisation. They involve getting better information for managing available resources, eliminating incentives to waste of resources, coordinating interdependent services more closely, and improving the assignment of responsibility for the way resources are used.

'The issues that must be faced in deciding how a nation's health services shall be organised, financed and administered entail many ideological and political value judgements concerning the proper roles of individuals, private and voluntary enterprise and the state. But policymakers in every country would be well-advised to ask themselves whether their systems can be improved against the four criteria we have described. Few,' he concludes, 'if they are honest in their questioning, will be wholly satisfied with the answers.'

THE PROCESS OF CHANGE

As Professor Margaret Scott Wright (1969) so rightly points out: 'Change . . . has become essential to the survival and development of all professional enterprise. It must therefore be recognised as a continuing process in which the team concept is vital.' The concept of change is the same for nurses and nursing as for all other professional groups.

Change is an alteration in the presently existing state or organisation. It may be a structural change in one's work framework involving a change of work place or in an organisational framework, such as occurred when the National Health Service was reorganised in 1974 or in the case of a home nurse whose duties are changed from caring for patients in a geographical area to caring for the patients of a single group of general practitioners. Structural changes often lead to a change in role for the nurse as her tasks and responsibilities often change with the structure. In other words changes in role functions often follow structural change in the organisation.

Closely associated with changes in function is a change in relationships as the changed structure often entails contact with different kinds of people.

It is a fairly common phenomenon for people to resist change: this is not always dysfunctional as there is in fact no necessary association between change and progress, even when the former is inevitable. Professor Scott Wright argues that: 'The impulse to resist change may indeed be correct on certain occasions. It is not always wise to follow current fashions or to climb on the bandwagon. One of the real problems in this field is to know when change is advisable and worth all the upheavel and disruption of people and processes involved.'

Change can either be imposed externally or can be accepted by a group or individual. Bendall (1973) argues that if structural change is imposed from without, functional change is less likely to follow than if it is accepted by the group because, apart from creating lack of commitment to the change process, problems related to 'vested power' and 'vested status' interests are created which not only hinder but can also block the change process.

Strategy for change

Both Bendall and Scott Wright stress the importance of effective communications before and during the change process, and Revans (1964) stresses the importance of communication as an essential expedient in effecting change in a number of studies of projects with which he has been associated. Outlining the project to nursing staff enhances their willingness and ability to appreciate the need for change.

The problem of implementation has to be solved long before any change process can be implemented and this, in Scott Wright's view, requires qualities of initiative, scientific knowledge and resilience. 'One of the most important principles is that the process of change is dependent upon the qualities and abilities of people.' The consent and understanding of those involved in the change process are essential and the originator of the idea must be able to communicate effectively.

Changes in health care service organisation cannot be brought about singlehanded and it is therefore important to involve people at all levels.

For change in nursing to be successful, Scott Wright suggests, that strong professional support from senior nurses is a useful ally but she warns that it does not necessarily guarantee success, as the non-implementation of the recommendations of a number of reports on nursing education demonstrates.

She maintains that it is often wise to 'allow time for the scars of a new idea to grow in less enlightened minds' and that certain important qualities are essential in those who are attempting to implement change; 'trained minds which understand the psychological and sociological as well as the scientific factors' associated with innovation of change, and ability to cope with 'the techniques of implementation and the measurements of the results achieved' in the change process.

Studies of change

The National Health Service was formally established in the United Kingdom in 1948. Up to that time, the hospital matron had functioned in a small, single, compact unit (Figure 7.2) and had been able to relate easily on a day-to-day basis with the medical superintendent and the hospital administrator. She had great oppor-

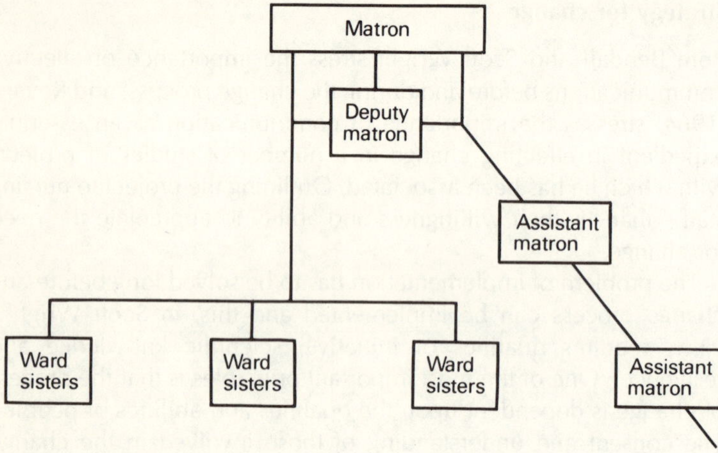

Figure 7.2 Nightingale nursing service organisation in the UK before 1948.

tunities for making the voice of the nursing staff heard, as each hospital had its own governing body.

After 1948, when the hospitals were grouped in single management groups, run by hospital management committees, this nursing voice was lost. Whereas the medical profession was assured a great deal of influence and control over hospital care (about a quarter of hospital management committees consisted of members of the medical profession), no provision was made for representation of nurses. Matrons were increasingly excluded from the complicated corridors of power. 'Either the matrons in the group had to meet together and select a spokesman to represent nursing at hospital management committee level, if such a spokesman were allowed, or take it in turns to attend, which in a large group would mean about once in two years' (Baly, 1973).

The *Report of the Committe on the Internal Administration of Hospitals* (1954) recommended that hospitals be administered on a day-to-day basis by a tripartite body consisting of a representative of the medical staff, the hospital administrator, and the matron. It also recommended that the matron should be able to report to the appropriate committees. Unfortunately, these recommendations were never fully implemented. There were no further dramatic changes for well over a decade.

In 1966, the *Report of the Committee on Senior Nursing Staff Structure,* was published, followed in 1969 by the *Report of the Working Party on Management Structure in the Local Authority*

Nursing Services. Both of these reports recommended that a chief executive post for nursing should be established for hospital (Figure 7.3) and community (Figure 7.4) nursing services. Each was to have

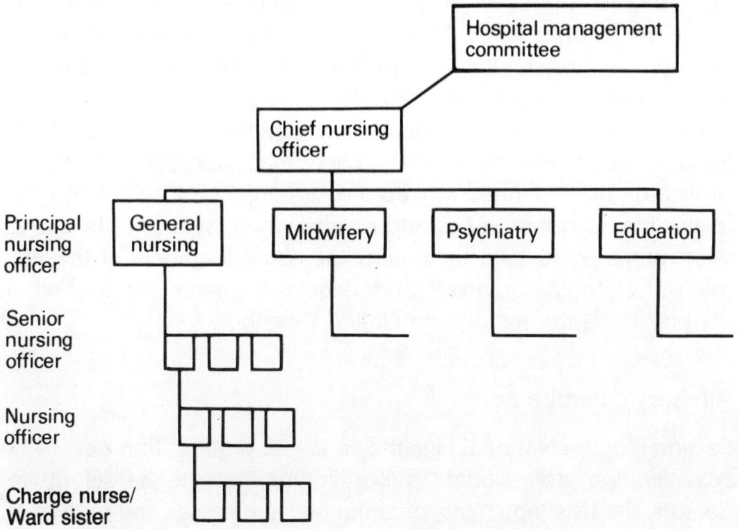

Figure 7.3 'Salmon' hospital nursing service organisation.

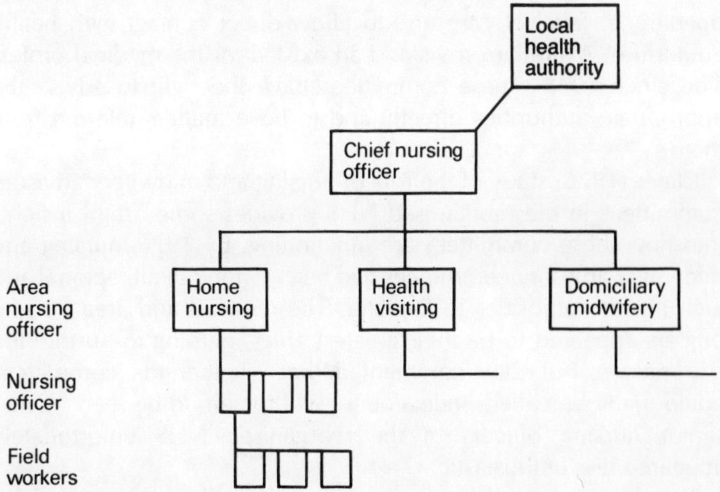

Figure 7.4 'Mayston' community nursing service organisation.

a chief nursing officer who would manage the nursing services and also have the right to participate in management committee meetings and be directly accountable to the management body. The recommendations of both reports were implemented and although considerable upheaval and some anxiety was created by the implementation, 'it could be that nursing administration will emerge in a more logical pattern that will enable it to fit more easily into an integrated service' (Baly, 1973).

Quite soon after the start of the newly integrated National Health Service, Scott Wright (1974) argued that, because the nursing profession in the United Kingdom had reorganised itself so quickly in the previous few years, and on the whole successfully, nurses were prepared to take their place as equal members of the new multi-disciplinary advisory and executive teams established at various levels throughout the United Kingdom.

Advisory committees

Section 8 of the National Health Service Re-organisation Act (1973) provided for professional advisory committees to be set up for doctors, dentists, opticians, pharmacists, and nurses and midwives. Following the reorganisation of the NHS in 1974, a nursing and midwifery advisory committee was established within each area and regional health authority in an attempt to get opinion from the operational level of care and to allow direct contact with health authorities. A similar provision had existed for the medical profession since 1948. These committees have the right to advise the appropriate authorities directly and to have matters referred from them.

Clay's (1976) study of the role of nursing and midwifery advisory committees in the reorganised NHS provides some useful insights into how these committees are functioning. By 1976, nursing and midwifery advisory committees had been formed in all regional and area health authorities in England. The regional and area nursing officers appeared to be their greatest allies, helping to nurture the committees. But Clay commented that whether the committees could really be called 'independent will remain to be seen'. Other senior nursing officers in the reorganised NHS unfortunately appeared less enthusiastic.

This study, as well as discussions with colleagues in the field, indicated that the number of 'grass root' members in each committee was very low indeed, and that this might affect their credibility. Since then, however, members have been elected by their peers, so that there is now some reason to believe that wide representation and proper balance will be achieved.

Clinical accountability

A most informative study of the change process in a health care organisation has been conducted by Wickings *et al.* (1975) at the Westminster Hospital, London. The project, an assessment of seven ward units of clinically accountable teams (doctors, nurses and administrators), was established to discover the effects of three organisational innovations.

'Firstly, ward staff received an information service about the resources they used on inpatient care; secondly, they were expected to manage budgets for their inpatient care responsibilities; thirdly they met regularly as clinically accountable teams to review the use of the resources they could control. Given the option of participating, five out of seven teams chose to hold regular meetings and made changes in their patterns of work. These changes were accompanied by an agreed redistribution of financial resources.'

The results of this project suggest that the potential for the participation of nurses in the change process in health care organisation appears to be exciting until the obvious medical dominance in the teams is noted. The project report documents how doctors, particularly the consultants, proposed most changes and, in fact, change did not take place unless it was acceptable to them.

'The nursing officers and administrators played little part in decision making at ward level. Ward sisters played a considerable role only when proposing reallocations of savings. They seemed to have only a minor role in agreeing changes at ward level.'

Change takes time

That organisational change is not an easy or speedy process is demonstrated by the fact that even legislation for change does not necessarily ensure that change will come about speedily—or at all—as is illustrated by events following the passing of the Mental Health Act of 1959 which, among other things, gave the (then) health authorities responsibilities for developing organised psychiatric care in the community. A review conference convened by the Royal Society of Health some nine years after legislation (Smith, 1968) demonstrated that the Act's philosophy had not been fully implemented due to a mixture of lack of finance, lack of research, lack of properly trained personnel and of some health authorities 'not shouldering their responsibilities under the 1959 Mental Health Act'. As a result, 'in parts of the country, community care existed only in theory. Family doctors appreciated the needs for such services but were left to cope . . .'

There is no evidence to suggest a rapid extension of this aspect of health care even after 1968, and because of concern about the apparent dearth of community care services for psychiatric patients the Queen's Nursing Institute commissioned a national research project to evaluate the state of affairs in 1974.

Education for change

'The concept of change and the possibility of measuring its effectiveness are principles which should be included in every student nurse programme and should be reinforced at all levels of the nurse's education, whether basic or post basic.' So contends Scott Wright—an argument with which I entirely concur. Some radical and controversial suggestions for education for change are proposed by Bendall.

In the first instance, Bendall argues, 'three existing processes' need to be completely reversed. The professional interests of status groups in the NHS must be displaced from the centre of the scene and replaced by the clients' interests. The dominance of nursing knowledge must be displaced to the periphery and nursing skills should be the centre of focus, which, she holds, will encourage schools of nursing to teach 'the management of real situations'. And the nursing educational system should change to put centrally the capacity for objective thinking. 'A nurse in training', Bendall argues, 'should not be provided with a stereotyped answer to meet a given situation, but with the capacity to reach different conclusions, having weighed up and evaluated all the components of each new situation.'

The implications of planning for change are great if this view is supported:

'First we have to re-educate the educators.'

'It involves a drastic rethinking of our hierarchy of status and salary.'

'It anticipates that those who now have power over the clinical nurse would need to learn not to command inferiors but to negotiate with equals.'

'It turns what are now regarded as ends (promotion to administration and teaching) into means to achieve the greater end of effective nursing.'

The comments should prove quite a challenge to nurse-sociologists of the future.

An example of organisational change

Following the introduction of legislation in Parliament *(note the political influence),* the largest reorganisation of health service organisation in Great Britain took place on 1st April 1974. The hospital services, previously managed by hospital management committees, were joined administratively to the community health services, previously managed by the local authorities. The implication of this organisational change for nursing was that, for the first time in the history of British health care, hospital and community nurses were to be responsible to the same nursing head. The authorities now responsible for all health services are the area and regional health authorities but the basic management unit is the district, of which there are one or more in each area. The district is based on a population of 100 000 to 400 000. In each district the health services are managed by a district management team consisting of a district administrator, a district finance officer, a district nursing officer, a district community physician together with one representative each of hospital medical consultants and the local general medical practitioners. These six people together manage the health services as 'co-equals' on a basis of 'consensus'. Each member has a right of veto, which means in practice that no one team member's view or opinion carries greater weight *per se* in discussion and no executive decision can be made unless all members concur. There can be no executive decision by majority vote.

The district management team meetings are chaired by one of the team members, usually on a rotation basis for a period of about six months (Table 7.1). The rotation of the chairmanship has a number of sociological functions in my view. It prevents the role developing

Table 7.1 Rotation of district management team chairmanship in Brent Health District

	1	2	3
Chairman	medical consultant	district administrator	general practitioner
Vice Chairman	district administrator	general practitioner	district nursing officer
	4	5	6
	district nursing officer	district community physician	district finance officer
	district community physician	district finance officer	medical consultant

into an executive role and therefore constantly endorses the co-equalness of team members. It also reduces the risk (and inherent dangers) of the routinisation of the personal charisma of any one team member in the role of chairman, which could arise if the chairmanship was held by any one person for a long period. The risk is also reduced of the routinisation of the role charisma of chairman in any one team member holding the role of chairman.

However, because of the large bureaucratic elements in the present health service organisation which are managed and coordinated on a day-to-day basis by the district administrator, there is a danger that that role could unwittingly emerge as a chief executive role which would be contrary to the philosophy and spirit of the concept of district management teams. Furthermore, if the reorganised health service is not evaluated and reviewed regularly there could be a danger that the goal of better resource utilisation for health care will be displaced by the goal of maintaining the organisation at all costs because of vested interests of office bearers.

AN EXECUTIVE ROLE FOR NURSES

In this new health service organisation nurses have been afforded an executive function in health service management that is unique in the world. It also ensures that nurses and nursing are controlled and managed by nurses as a professional right (Smith 1979).

I joined the reorganised health service as a district nursing officer on 1st April 1974 in the Brent Health District (200 000 population) and it has afforded me an involvement with organisational change, some details of which are documented below.

Changing the nursing service management organisation

I shall restrict the discussion to the changes in the nursing service management organisation, with particular reference to the hospital nursing services which were changed from an institutionally managed service to a functionally managed service.

Prior to reorganisation the hospital nursing services in Brent (one large and three small hospitals) had been managed on a day-to-day basis by senior nursing officers purely on a institutional basis. In hospital A, the two senior nursing officers had functioned under global titles of 'medical' and 'surgical', but the former also had responsibilities for geriatric nursing and the latter for theatre and emergency departments. In hospitals B, C, and D the senior nursing officers managed all nursing services very much on a site coordinator basis. There was also a senior nursing officer (staff post) who had acted as professional assistant to the former chief nursing officer (Figure 7.5).

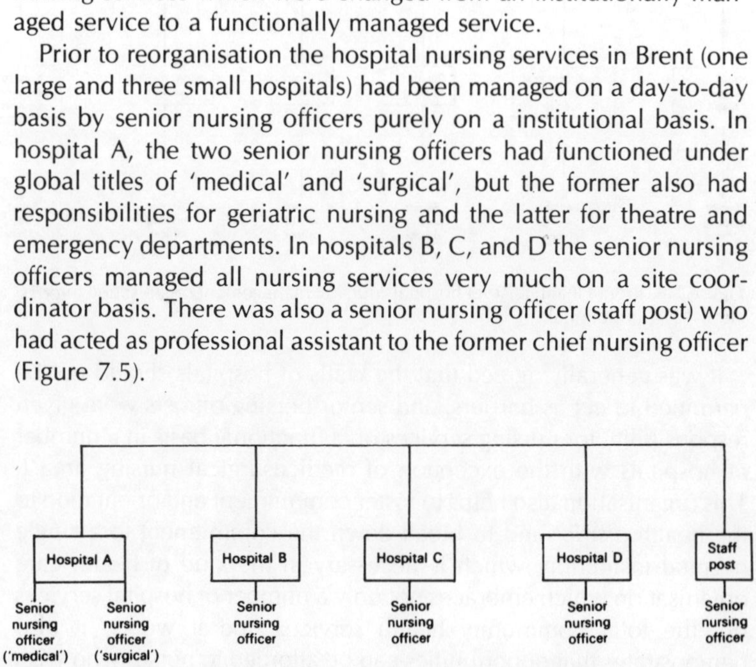

Figure 7.5 Brent Health District hospitals nursing management organisation prior to 1st April 1974 (institutional).

Believing strongly that nurse managers should be primarily responsible for managing *nursing* according to their own clinical orientation, the district nursing officer devised an organisational plan for functional management by senior nursing officers *(note the ideological influence)*.

There was a further influence on the organisational structure, namely a financial one. The new organisation had not to cost any more than the previous one.

After much discussion by senior nursing staff in groups and individually with the district nursing officer, and a number of informal discussions between the district nursing officer and district management team colleagues, the proposed organisational structure was devised after a series of three drafts (Figure 7.6).

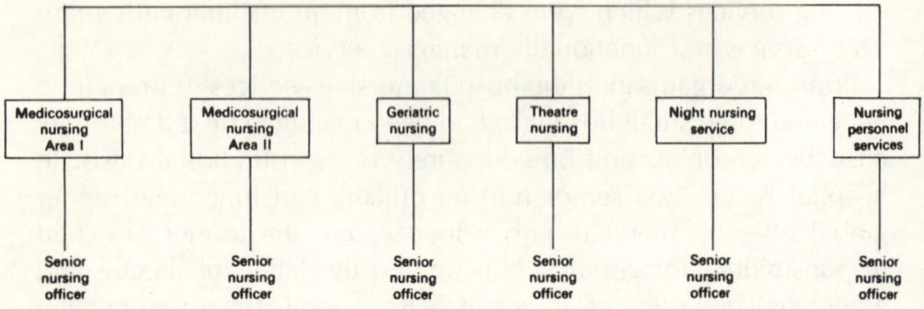

Figure 7.6 Brent Health District hospitals nursing management organisation after 1st April 1974 (functional).

It was generally agreed that the walls of hospitals should not be permitted to act as barriers, and senior nursing officers were given responsibility for nursing services on a functional basis in a number of hospitals with the exception of medicosurgical nursing area I. This organisation also helps to foster commitment and orientation to the health *district* and to break down the commitment to a single hospital institution, which is necessary in the kind of health care organisation which embraces not only a number of hospital services but the total community health service. And it works; it also demonstrates that opportunities can be afforded to nurses who wish to progress professionally along a *clinical* route if the appropriate organisation is devised. In my view, the organisation of nursing service management should always be a means to the end of maintaining excellence in *nursing*. The organisation should never be permitted to become an end in itself and encourage nurses to make a fetish out of management for its own sake.

An evolutionary process

Planning and innovating the change also confirmed that change really is an evolutionary process.